THE EMPLOYER IN YOU

SERIES: NO 1

REPOSITIONING YOURSELF FROM HAVING AN EMPLOYEE MIND TO HAVING AN EMPLOYER MIND

You, like the bird in a cage, have untapped potential of an employer yearning to be released. All you need is repositioning your mind

SIMON MBUYI KAYEKESI

THE EMPLOYER IN YOU

SERIES: NO1

REPOSITIONING YOURSELF FROM HAVING AN EMPLOYEE MIND TO HAVING AN EMPLOYER MIND

SIMON MBUYI KAYEKESI

© 2017 Simon Mbuyi Kayekesi

All rights reserved. This book, or parts thereof, may not be reproduced in any form without permission from the publisher; exceptions made for brief excerpts used in published reviews.

Contact: skayekesi@gmail.com

      +260977448398

      oscar.yopa@gmail.com

      +260978133368

ACKNOLEDGEMENT

Special thanks to the Almighty God, El Shaddai, my Father, the one to whom I owe all that I have become and are yet to become. He is the one who has worked in me and my family to reach a level where we are able to create, make and establish things and also come up with the ideas that are shared in this book beyond my wildest imagination. My gratitude to my wife Queen who kept on encouraging and asking me when the book would be published. This made me put in the best I could. My children whom I spent time communicating the insights to and responded to the challenge of them releasing the employer in them have been inspiring. They have been partners with me on this journey to provoking ourselves and the world on the Employer In You insight.

My appreciation goes to Pastor Godfrey Kashweka who kept on inspiring me to reach out beyond my boundaries. Thanks also to Mr. Paul Lupunga who kept on reminding me that I had the ability to put the ideas I had into books and other media-this one being one of them. Special thanks to my Nephew Oscar Yopa who has been my assistant and co- worker in making the book taken to the market and managing the marketing process. My nephew Clement Mayamba who designed the book cover deserves special thanks. Special thanks to my nephew Mapesho Kamayani who kept telling me that the book needed to be published. Special thanks also to my daughter Jireh Kayekesi and her colleague Kahinga Chiweyi for inspiring me when they came up with a **freezits** machine that added value to the insights on the Employer in You. Jireh kept on encouraging me to make my potential released in order to bless many. I say thanks. **Thanks to the following Men of God from whom I have learned a lot: Pastor Myles Munroe (posthumous), Pastor Sam Adeyemi, Pastor Mensah Otabil, Bishop T.D.Jakes, Pastor David Abioyemie, Dr. John Maxwell, Bishop David Oyedepo, Pastor Mathew Ashimolowo.** By listening to these men of God and others, I have been able to compare some of the teachings I developed before listening to them and validated my work.

My thanks also go to the following I have listened to people and have motivated me: Mr. Les Brown, Ms. Terri Savelle Foy, Mr. Bob Proctor and the late Mr. Jim Rohn, Mr. Tony Robbins, Mr. John Assaraf and Mr. Marcus

Buckingham who have motivated me even more to do what I am doing now. My thanks go to all those who initially listened to my sharing on this subject and encouraged me to take the message further. I give thanks to all of you the millions of potential beneficiaries of this series and the others to come who, despite not talking to me in person, made me have a feeling that you were waiting for this book. It is the consciousness of you clients out there that fired up the passion within me in writing this book.

DEDICATION

Dedicated to Jesus in whom is hidden treasures of wisdom and knowledge who has worked in me to reposition myself to having an employer mind.

PREFACE

"You cannot travel within and stand still without." James Allen Applying this quote to the employer in You insights, we can learn a lot from the repositioning that took place in the mind of Jacob. This mind repositioning led to transformation in the economic position of Jacob from having an employee mind to having an employer mind. Recent meditation on Romans12:2 revealed four key elements that are important in repositioning which Jacob could have gone through in transforming himself from being an employee to being an employer namely: (1). Not being conformed to the world standards which include employee mentality (2). The need for Mind renewal (3). Transformation taking place as a result of mind renewal (4). Transformation resulting in you and me proving the good, acceptable and perfect will of God for our lives.

Before approaching uncle Laban to release him from working for him for many years, it looks like Jacob had travelled far within himself. He had travelled in his mind in an endeavour to become an employer after being an employee for many years. The man could have traversed distances in his mind and imagined what his situation could be if he repositioned himself. Finally after travelling inside, he was able to travel without. His situation and his outlook changed without. This was after changing within confirming what the Bible says in Proverbs23:7 that as a man thinks so is he. It confirmed the fact that you are a reflection of what you are inside. Jacob's change in thinking that took place as a result of mind renewal resulted in him finally becoming an employer. **The same can be true for you and me by repositioning taking place in our minds to become employers.** This is what the insights on the Employer in You, arranged and presented in series of which this is the first series, is all about. I trust that reading this book will lead you into repositioning yourself to become what God intended you to be –an employer.

Simon Mbuyi Kayekesi

Contents

INTRODUCTION: 1

CHAPTER 1: WASTED EMPLOYER POTENTIAL 5

CHAPTER2: THE LAW OF PLACE (THE LAW OF POSITIONING) 15

CHAPTER3: THE EMPLOYER IN YOU 19

CHAPTER4: NOT COMFORMING TO WORLD PATTERNS AND MIND RENEWAL KEY TO TRANSFORMATION 49

CHAPTER5: REPOSITIONING YOURSELF FROM HAVING AN EMPLOYEE MIND TO HAVING AN EMPLOYER MIND 70

CHAPTER6: HIGHLIGHTS ON MY REPOSITIONING MYSELF AND MY FAMILY TO HAVING EMPLOYER MINDS 76

CHAPTER7: THE POWER OF THE MIND IN REPOSITIONING YOURSELF 87

CHAPTER8: RELEASING THE EMPLOYER IN YOU 97

CHAPTER9: THE EMPLOYER IN YOU AND THE DOMINION CYCLE 111

CHAPTER10: ON A JOURNEY TO DOMIMION AS AN EMPLOYER (AN ENTREPRENUER) 117

CHAPTER11: THE 3 INGREDIENTS FOR BUILDING, ESTABLISHING AND FILLING (POPULATING) YOUR BUSINESS HOUSE 127

CHAPTER 12: THE IMPORTANCE OF VALUE IN THE MARKET PLACE 132

CHAPTER13: DEVELOPING YOUR PRODUCT OR SERVICE TO TAKE TO THE MARKET 136

CHAPTER14: MARKETING YOUR PRODUCT OR FRUIT 148

INTRODUCTION:

THE TRAPPED EMPLOYER INSIDE YOU

Trapped inside each one of us is an employer yearning to be released. There is an employer in you yearning to be released from the trap of being an employee. *God made us employers*. But alas, many of us end up being employees without realizing the employer in us that God made us to be. We find ourselves, as the late Man of God Myles Munroe put it, *doing jobs we do not enjoy for the sake of a salary or a wage*. Even for those who enjoy their jobs, most of them are in such jobs simply for sustenance and they spend most of their lives working hard to get only little compared to their input. *Each one of us is carrying a child inside us wanting to be given birth to or we die with the child in us called an employer. To do so there is need for repositioning to take place in our minds. There is an employer in you waiting for you to reposition your mind to become one.* Remember that it is employers who are smarter than employees because they benefit from the dividends and have employees looking to them for their survival. *Decide to think and act like an employer and enjoy the freedom and benefits it comes with.*

Clearly the majority of people are on the employee side where they sell their labour for a pay. The few who are employers pay the employees in order for them to add value to their means of production. As a result the employers make profits using employees and ultimately get paid from dividends while employees get paid from cost of production (wages). *The difference as we shall establish in this book is in the way we all think.* It is either your thinking is that of an employer or that of an employee. Those who think like employers end up doing things of their own and end up employing those who have employee minds. *As the law of sowing and reaping states, the employer and the employee end up reaping proportionate to what they have been sowing.* One who has sown capital including the other means of production, ends up reaping dividends and the one who has been sowing labour ends up reaping wages. This is a law whose implication makes differences in the lives of people in society. Having worked as an employee for many years, I concluded that *it pays to reposition oneself in your mind and take the side of an employer to benefit from being an employer*. The advantages of being on an employer side are enormous.

WHAT LED TO THESE INSIGHTS?

These insights came as a result of my many years of study and sharing on the life of Abraham, Isaac and Jacob as portrayed and written in the Bible. My study especially of Genesis30:25-43 and Genesis31 made me realize what it means to be an employer as opposed to being an employee. This came to my mind when I compared the life of Jacob in the same environment for many years but with two different types of results in his life. The first part of his life was before Genesis30:25 when he worked hard and he was the man behind Laban's business growth but ended up having wages simply for sustenance. The second was after Genesis30:25. What I saw from verse 25 to verse 43 was dramatic for a man who for over fourteen years lived a life of a poor hard working man. The total numbers years Jacob worked for Laban was twenty years according to Genesis31:38. But *the turnaround that took place in the remaining years out of the twenty years made me ask as to what made the difference.* The conclusion I made resulted in me coming up with these series of books entitled: The Employer in You.

Even if Jacob became an employee, there was already an employer in him yearning to be released. *The problem that made him have the results he got was in his mind. He had positioned his mind as an employee and the results he got according to the law that governs what an employee reaps had to work in his life. When he repositioned himself in his mind as an employer, the law that governs what an employer reaps had to work in the same man called Jacob in the same environment.* This made me conclude that what made the difference in the results he got in the two phases of his economic crisis and his economic boom respectively was about positioning. *When he changed his positioning, beginning with his mind, his behaviour changed and results followed suit. This drastic change in his economic status was to his wonder of what God can do when a man or woman positions himself or herself rightly.* This can also be a wonder to me and it can also be a wonder to you when we rightly position ourselves. Now where was Jacob all along before Genesis30:25? This is something worth taking note as you read this book.

Further my experience working as an employee for over 25 years made me see myself in Jacob as an employee. The challenges I faced in life as an employee for many years made me make a decision to reposition myself with the mind of an employer as opposed to having the mind of an employee. In this regard, I have written these insights as one who carried an employee mind for many years until when *I came to my senses that there was an employer in me yearning to be released.* It is this light that shone in my heart and brought about transformation in my life that resulted in me doing some things that I never dreamed I could ever do in my life. Among them composing and singing gospel music and writing this Book to be marketed to the world as a global marketer.

THE BASIS OF THE INSIGHTS

As pointed out above, I have developed this teaching based on the insights I got from the study of Genesis30:25-43 and Genesis 31 and also from personal experience as a government employee for over 25 years. These verses teach us about *the steps that Jacob took to reposition himself from having an employee mind to having an employer mind which led to a turnaround in his life regarding wealth creation*.

Jacob a man who started as an employee transformed himself to become an employer. What was the secret? *The secret was in repositioning himself in his mind and then him having an idea that he finally implemented.* What made a difference this time with the earlier years that Jacob spent in Laban's enterprise before things turned around? The difference was in conforming himself to the employee standard and the lack of mind renewal that constrained transformation from taking place in his economic situation. This time, after refusing to conform to employee standard and deciding to reposition himself in his mind, his results changed after Genesis30:25 going forward. *The result of the change in his type of thinking was wealth creation as recorded in Genesis30:43*. He experienced a turnaround resulting from repositioning.

THE MOTIVATION FOR SHARING THESE INSIGHTS

Having come to an understanding that there is trapped in each one of us an employer, *I have developed the insights so that I may motivate some people to realize the employer in them*. The motivation for my sharing these insights is, therefore, to provoke your thoughts that you may make a decision to reposition yourself from having an employee mind to having an employer mind. It is also to encourage those who, like me, have already decided to reposition themselves in their minds to be employers. Further, I have developed the teaching so that I can share these insights with other people who might have gone through a similar situation like mine and possibly provoke them unto love and good works-*provoke them to reposition themselves with the mind of an employer.*

By sharing these insights, especially with the youth starting with those in my household, I have a conviction that I will perhaps win some of them to make a decision to position themselves from the very beginning as employers instead of being employees. This will help nations when the number of those in the private sector increases especially at the time when unemployment is a serious challenge that governments are grappling with. Sharing these insights is as a result of my realization that there could be some youths who need to be availed with such type of information which people like me did not have during our youth. I only have got such knowledge as I am about to retire and wishing I had acquired it earlier. How I wish I had got such insights earlier though I believe it is never too late for me.

The insights can also be an encouragement to those who have already repositioned themselves who can use them to sharpen what they already have. The most important source of motivation for sharing these insights is that I have a similar motivation like the one Apostle Paul in the Bible had to tell Timothy to entrust the word of God to reliable men who should be qualified to teach others. As the late man of God Myles Munroe put it, the most important aspect of leadership is where you leave a successor to carry on with your vision. As is the case with relay, where you give a baton to another to continue with the race, we need *to pass it on to those who get the revelation and carry on with the insights to impact current and future generations.* In this regard, it is also my heart's desire to pass on such insights to those who may take them forward so that I die empty and leave a legacy behind.

MY DREAM ABOUT THIS BOOK

As I design these insights, I am conscious of you among the millions of potential beneficiaries of the insights and the others to come who, *despite some of you not talking to me in person, made me have a feeling that you were waiting for this book to unlock the employer potential in you. It is this consciousness of you beneficiaries out there that fired up the passion within me to design these insights* and share them in order for me to give a gift to the world by having a positive impact by realizing employers around the world.

I am convinced that, by you reading beyond this page, you too will be encouraged by *the insights that have revolutionized my thinking from having an employee mind to having an employer mind.* I hope and trust that you also will get the revelation I got and even be provoked to take steps that you might have not thought of taking. My dream is that these insights be of positive impact to the whole world as the insights will be shared across the globe to bring about repositioning in the minds of many people so that they become what God already gave them called dominion to fulfil Genesis1:26-28, Genesis9:1,7 and Psalms8: 4-6 to the glory of God.

CHAPTER 1: WASTED EMPLOYER POTENTIAL

THE BIRD IN A CAGE-LOCKED UP POTENTIAL TO FLY

Being an employee instead of being an employer is a depiction of wasted employer potential. It is like a bird which was created to fly higher and farther but is locked up in a cage. This is a bird with great potential to fly but its potential is limited by being in a cage. What is depicted in the picture below is a picture of a bird in a cage. ***What comes into your mind as you look at the picture is locked up potential of a bird which is supposed to fly higher and farther.*** It is a picture of a bird that I got from the Island of Bali in Indonesia when I went there to attend the World Trade Organization Conference.

FIGURE1: THE BIRD LOCKED UP IN A CAGE WITH POTENTIAL TO FLY HIGHER AND FURTHER

What is presented below is the email containing the message that I sent to the Manager of the hotel whom I requested to photograph the birds he kept in a cage at the hotel in Bali Indonesia. I responded to him after I had a chat with him and I requested him to capture the pictures and share them with me which he then emailed to me:

Dear ...,

Thank you very much for the photos on the birds that you have kept in a cage. They look health and active and they wish to fly out of the cage, but unfortunately they cannot reach their potential by flying higher and farther. This is because the cages do not have openings that are big enough to allow then to fly out and fly higher and farther to reach their highest potential.

I must say that this is an unforgettable lesson that I have learned from your hotel as I shared with you briefly regarding the law of expansion as written by Mr. John C. Maxwell in his book: The 15 Invaluable Laws of Growth. It has made me reflect on my life and realize that I am like the birds in a cage who could have flown farther and higher but seem to be held up in a cage. I am always wishing to 'fly' higher and farther like an aeroplane that goes to a higher altitude to easy its flying but don't seem to 'fly' as I should. I hope that you also, being the first person I have shared this insight with, can learn something from it as you look at those birds in a cage. I believe I can 'fly' higher and farther.

I recall in the discussion between you and me regarding the hotel when I asked if you only have 12 rooms you responded, "Yes, small is good." But as you can recall I reminded you that to some extent yes small may be good but ultimately God made us with the ability to expand. And you agreed with me that big things start small.

To make this point clearer, let me share with you an additional insight on this. In my country Zambia, we have the Zambezi River whose source comes from my home area. It is from the Zambezi River that we derive the country's name. When you go to the source of the Zambezi River, you see a little amount of water coming from below the roots of a fallen tree that has been lying on the ground for many years. However, though the first thing you see is little water flowing downstream, you can also see that the source is in a deep trough (furrow or channel) which sends a message to one's mind that a big thing is yet to come out from this small looking source.

To sum up, the Zambezi River starts small but ends up being one of the biggest rivers in Africa and the world. When you see it a few kilometres farther, near my home village, it even has some rapids and currently someone put up a hydro power station supplying power to this rural area of Zambia. The River further flows into Angola, then back into Zambia in Chavuma District. It goes further to make borders between Zambia and Namibia, Botswana and Zimbabwe until it enters Mozambique and finally takes its waters to the Indian Ocean. It is on the Zambezi River that you find the Victoria Falls in Southern Africa and one of the biggest man-made lakes in the world called Lake Kariba.

Isn't this amazing? A river that starts from the roots of a fallen tree but having such potential for expansion to the extent that I believe the Zambezi River in a way contributes some drops of water to the ocean where Bali, Indonesia is!

So what is the lesson from the Zambezi River? **BIG THINGS START SMALL.** As you rightly put it in our discussion even us as human beings are born as small babies but transform into adults-this is growth. But beyond this physical growth into adults, each one of us has the potential to expand farther and fly higher by "flying" like the birds in a cage beyond "our cages".

I hope that, like me, these insights will provoke you into expansion to go further than believing that "Small is better" or put another way like the case of the birds in cages to " fly" higher and farther than saying "the cages are better".

Regards

Simon Kayekesi

Zambia.

As you can deduce from the above email message, by you looking at the bird in a cage, you will realize that in Genesis 1:20, God created birds to fly above the earth in the skies. When you consider the bird in a cage above, you can see a bird who's potential to fly higher and farther, according to God's purpose, is locked up in a cage. The picture tells us that having potential is one thing and releasing it to the extent that it is maximized to fulfil one's original purpose is another. The bird in the cage flies around in the cage but the extent to which it flies is limited. God made the bird to fly in a wide environment and to fly higher and farther. And yet its ability to fly was limited by the environment in which it found itself. Interesting enough, the owner said he had tried to release the bird when he saw it struggling to fly out but after four days it came back and he ever since locked it in the cage again. Why did it go back to the cage? Its mind was conditioned to be in the cage such that it did not realize that the cage was not its best. Despite God's purpose for it to fly, it was not flying. It was misplaced, misused and its purpose not fully realized. What a tragedy!

Once again, I saw myself as one who had acknowledged the potential in me but was not doing what I believe I was born to do. I was risking myself being buried with all that potential in me to 'fly' in an environment that gives me more space. One of the areas that I have seen my potential locked up is in the area of my being an employee. *I have a lot of brilliant ideas but I have been failing to apply them because of the environment in which I have found myself in and because of my thinking* for the past over twenty five years that I have been an employee. *My thinking has had a big impact on the results I have got in life-lack of satisfaction and meaning.* When we realize that we were not meant for the cage but to fly out there and make a decision to move out of the cage, we get satisfaction and fulfilment. *I have come to realize that yearning inside me is an employer locked up in a cage as an employee.* Like the bird in a cage, being an employee is not the best for me. I have potential to 'fly' higher and farther if I repositioned myself by coming out of the cage of an employee and fly higher and farther as an employer realising the God given potential in me. That could be the case for you as well. *That potential in you is to be an employer rather than being an employee.*

THERE IS AN EMPLOYER IN YOU

God wired each one of us with the capacity to work and work for ourselves as employers. When I analyse Ephesians4:28, it simply says that if you were stealing stop. It says stop stealing and work with your own hands so as to have something for yourself and something to share with someone in need. The scripture does not say get employed. It simply says work with your own hands. The situation is that God wired each one of us with the capacity to work for ourselves. The scripture says work with your own hands. Working with your hands does not necessarily say you become an employee neither does it say become an employer. It is an open ended statement leaving you and I with a choice to make as to which side we take. Though the majority take the employee side, you could be among those few who can work using your hands as an employer and employ those who cannot think for themselves.

WE WERE TAUGHT ONLY ONE PATH-BECOMING EMPLOYEES

For most of us, we were simply taught one path which was that you go to v school and after school you get employed. Yes it sounded good but personally after acquiring the knowledge, in old age, that there is the other side of being an employer. I wish I could be a youth again and take the path of being an employer. Robert Kiyosaki in his book Before You Quit Your Job says that many parents tell their children to go to school so that they can get a good job. He says that he is yet to hear any parent who says to a child to go school to become an entrepreneur. At least he is able to find me. Ever since I got the revelation from these insights, I have been sharing with my children, with passion, that they may choose to become employers and avoid going the root I took of becoming an employee. I thank God that at the time of this writing, I have already won the hearts of some of them. It is for this same reason that I share this revelation in order to be among those who will take the path of becoming an employer that many of us were never taught. This is the major motivation for this book.

THE ENVIRONMENT IN WHICH I FOUND MYSELF AS A PROVOCTION ARENA

When I moved from a classroom as a teacher to become a statistician and later a Senior Education Planner, I had some form of satisfaction with the achievements I thought I had accomplished. Beyond this I yearned for further promotion. This was to some extent some obsession on my part looking at how hard I worked. Of course I later got promoted to a higher position. Interesting enough, it took me many years without getting promoted again up to the time of this writing despite knowing that I had potential to occupy higher positions. During this period, I desired to be promoted and efforts to promote me came my way but somehow I did not get promoted. Meanwhile, I felt that I deserved being promoted and yet nothing was materializing. I saw others I thought were less capable than I being promoted. I got dissatisfied with this status quo especially after stock taking of what I had within me, around me and beyond me. During this period, I started getting these insights that have become a treasure to me. I thank God that all things work together for good to those who love Him and are called for His purpose. My not being promoted created room for me to get these insights that I am now sharing with you and others. Thank God that now this desire for promotion has since disappeared. I now yearn to promote myself as an employer. Since 2012, I embarked on self-development with a view of promoting myself instead of waiting for others to promote me. This journey has been so satisfying and fulfilling.

Having been brought up in a village and later did most of my working career in the rural area, one of those things I desired to see happen was for me to fly on an aeroplane. Thank God that He gives us the desires of our hearts when we delight in Him. When I moved to another position and got into town, my new position required me to travel abroad and I found myself flying several times. At least this desire was fulfilled. Despite a few things that seemed to tell me that I had achieved by moving to a higher position, I realized that in essence, I had been taken some steps backwards in terms of the job content of my new position. This was so despite the new position being higher in terms of pay compared to my previous work. I found myself doing more of executive work of drafting letters where the whole day would be spent by making corrections on the letters I had drafted as they went through the bureaucracy. This was despite me being a holder of a Diploma and Advanced Diploma in Mathematics Teaching, a Degree in Economics Major and Minor in Public Administration, a Master's Degree in Economic Policy Management and then about to graduate with a Doctorate in Business Administration. What I was doing from 08 00 hours to 17 00 hours was not in tune with the skills and abilities that I had.

I looked at my talents and skills that I had but were packed in an office for the sake of a salary and a trip to travel abroad! I wanted to run away to avoid this type of work by going to some other Department or ministry but my effort failed for a period of over seven years. As already pointed out above, there sometimes were some openings that came my way but somehow the openings closed. I continued for over seven years in the same position and same type of uninteresting work until when this provocation to have an employer mind came upon my mind. Thank God for this revelation. As a result, I have been working on this insight ever since. The insights provoked me into *developing these teachings to stir me into action and deciding that I needed to share these insights with my family and beyond my family*. I made this decision so that the employer mind would be realized in me and them. You could be one of those these insights are meant for.

THE AGONY OF AN EMPLOYEE

Let us look at the agony of an employee. Sometimes, the master may tell you to sit at the same point for hours doing nothing. Within your heart you would know that you are *wasting very important resources called time and potential which is made idle* while in the name of loyalty, whose reward is a salary or a wage. Despite doing nothing, you end up sitting where the master has said sit.

Even if the master has not told you to sit, you yourself out of loyalty and being afraid of losing your pay want to make sure you please your master by sitting down waiting for instruction from the master, the employer. This is the agony of the servant, the employee-having all the potential, the time, the opportunities, the ideas squandered by the employer.

The worst thing for you as an employee is when some ***wonderful ideas are crying within you to be birthed and bring about change*** but your boss who is bereft of knowledge and incompetent is not willing to support your brilliant ideas. ***The boss, be it the owner of the organization or your supervisor, will only go with you to the extent of his or her capacity to comprehend what you are communicating***. When he or she reaches the maximum which my former pupils that I taught mathematics used to call reaching end of thinking capacity (ETC), the boss would not be willing to go where you would wish you took the organization. ***As long as you continue being an employee under such a boss, your ideas will not go anywhere***. You are doomed as an employee. ***The best option is to have your own enterprise and apply your brilliant ideas there. Many of us have buried our brilliant ideas in the graveyard called employee position.*** This is agony as *we may end up being buried with these ideas*. At least with this truth and going forward, I believe you will join me in deciding to ***apply our brilliant ideas in our own business undertakings as employers.***

FROM ECONOMIST TO PROTOCOL OFFICER-WASTAGE OF POTENTIAL

I had a nasty experience while out on duty which I have called the agony of an employee when as an economist I was questioned for not doing the work of a protocol officer. This is not to underrate or undermine the honourable job of a protocol officer. It is about the misuse of a resource that is meant for another function. What happened is that I was questioned by the delegation leader on the part of experts why I was not doing protocol work for one of the ministers who was part of our delegation. The interesting thing is that the Minister had travelled with a protocol officer who was attending to him but I was questioned as to why I was not attending to him.

To me this was a surprise because I knew that I was not a Protocol Officer but an Economist. I responded by telling the delegation leader that I was an expert to give expert advice and not to do protocol work. Of course if there was no Protocol Officer I would then come in but not where the Protocol Officer was available. This day ***I was disturbed to imagine how man had undervalued my worth***. Being reduced from economist to protocol officer was the last straw that struck my back regarding the insights on the employer in me. *Failure by human beings to see value in you and determine how best they can utilize you as a resource makes them use you for a wrong thing. How on earth can I be misplaced, misused, misguided, underutilized, underestimated and wrongly deployed!* Any way those who have misused me may not be the ones to blame. *I am the one to blame given the employee thinking that I have had for years.* To me having an employee mind has cost me a lot in life. Man's failure to utilize me as a resource appropriately risked making me useless if I did not take actions to reposition myself in my mind as an employer.

THE MISUSE OF WHAT YOU ARE PREGNANT WITH

Cardinal in the whole of this story is *the realization that I was being underutilized by my employer given what I was pregnant with, coupled with the feeling of emptiness in me in terms of not leaving a fulfilled life*. I realized that society can place you in a place where you don't belong. But thank God that *like a caterpillar, we have the ability to transform ourselves into butterflies by coming out of the shell*. I realized that complaining was useless as it was turning out to be a trap for me and it was not going to help. *I then made a resolve to start dreaming and imagining what I could do with what I already had within and without to make me start creating wealth*. I had to start creating value given what I had acquired so far. Thank God for the knowledge, the experience, the skills and the abilities that I have acquired so far. This is wealth to me as *I see myself as a rich man*.

As I am sharing the insights I am *speaking as one who has repositioned his mind. My mind has travelled far beyond my work place. I see an employer in me.* How I wish these insights became clearer to me much earlier! However, I have got encouragement that it may never be too late for me, as well as for any of you, *to reposition myself*.

In the actual sense my reliable source of encouragement comes from the Bible in Psalms 92:12-15 which tells me that the righteous will continue being fruitful even in old age. Now above fifty three years old, I have to *focus my fruitfulness towards bringing out the employer who is already in me*. I feel it is not too late for me. You can do the same and reposition yourself. As Les Brown puts it say yes to your dreams and reposition yourself to accomplish your dreams as an employer. He says we have got power to change our direction by taking calculated risks.

THE SECURITY MAN'S PARADOX

As we were in a queue waiting to go in to attend the opening of African Union Summit in South Africa, I had a chat with two colleagues from Ghana whose first names were Anthony and Patrick respectively. Earlier Patrick heard me share my thought on what I entitled the Agony of an employee. When we met again another time, he started the discussion making his colleague Anthony join.

Key in this chat was what Anthony said which I have termed "the Security Man's Paradox". He talked of a security man who leaves ten children and his wife to go and guard one person who is alone. He leaves his family in the hands of God to go and guard this one person. The rich man will be inside while him as a security man would be outside. I then added and said, "So it means that he put not only his family but himself as well at risk for a pay? This is really the agony of an employee." Imagine the time you have stayed idle doing nothing at your work place when you actually know that if you walked out to go and do one or two things, you would make a difference in your life. But because the master has stipulated that you have to report at a particular time and knock off at a particular time, what matters is for you to be in office sometimes doing nothing but having complied with the master's instruction or rules.

When we question the way our time, potential, skills and knowledge are utilized, we will realize that we could do much better than what we do under the instructions of the master.

GOD IS LIKE AN EAGLE AND I AM LIKE AN EAGLET

Growth and Comfort never coexist – F0rbes

Thank God that Deutoronomy32:11-14, says God is like an eagle and I am like an eaglet. He made me find myself in this environment which in my opinion was the most horrifying working environment I ever found myself in. This is despite all the good things I encountered by being in my current position. Now I have an urge within me saying that just as an eaglet's being made to fly out of the comfortable nest, I have an eagle in me. Like an eaglet maturing into an eagle able to fly and the mother forces them out of the nest, I needed to quit the comfort of a nest and act like an eagle by flying higher and further. You also need to do the same. *There is an eagle in you waiting to fly higher and further and be what God made you to be.*

THE MOTIVATION TO 'FLY' LIKE AN EAGLE

The outcome of my stay in the environment I have described, with the many other trials I faced that I have not highlighted, have given me valuable insights that are worth sharing with the world. Further my study of the life of Jacob as narrated in Genesis30 and Genesis31 has made me realize that ***we can change our current status of being poor to being rich by repositioning our minds.*** This is what has motivated me to do what I am doing now in my personal life and decided to share these insights that may be of value to someone out there. It has motivated me to fly like an eagle and realize my dreams. One of the fulfilment of my dreams is writing this book. You could be that person these insights were meant for. If that be the case, I am encouraged and blessed as a result. ***You need to move from your 'cage' of comfort and 'fly' like an eagle.***

CHAPTER 2: THE LAW OF PLACE (THE LAW OF POSITIONING)

This Book is about repositioning yourself from having an employee mind to having an employer mind. ***Before we talk about repositioning, we have to first talk about positioning. There is what I call the law of the place or the law of positioning.*** The position in which you are means quite a lot to what you get or end up becoming. I got this insight of the law of position or the law of place from 1Kings17:2-16 where we read about Elijah being in two places and the results being different in the two places. While in a place called Cherith that is after Jordan, God used ravens to feed Elijah and he drunk from a brook. After sometime, the brook dried. Thereafter, God told Elijah to go to Zarephath and in this place God met the needs of Elijah in a different way. Here God used a widow to meet the needs of Elijah while the widow benefited from taking care of Elijah.

I saw that there is a law that operates in terms of different places which I have called the law of the place. In one place he had the experience of ravens feeding him while in the other he had the experience of a widow with food enough for a meal only to die thereafter. After taking a step of faith to share the last meal with Elijah, the provision never dried. This is what happens with the location you take. Look at football. When players on the pitch are playing, all of them have chances of scoring but the one in the box has higher chances. The position you play affects your results to a great extent. This law of place has an impact on the results each one of us gets at the end of the day. In what place are you located physically or in terms of your mind?

The following are some of the other examples which can illustrate the law of positioning at work:

THE LAW OF PLACE - ABRAHAM POSITIONED HIMSELF IN HIS MIND AS AN EMPLOYER

God's taking Abraham outside in Genesis 15 was to make Abraham reposition himself from being an exalted father to being a father of many nations. He wanted Abraham to have a multiplier mind and be a distributor of his abilities. He wanted him to have a mentality of someone who was to have children like sand on the seashore and like stars on in the universe. God tells Abraham to see and tells him to walk east, west, north and south. He told Abraham to see and to walk in all directions to find a location for his tent. He gave Abraham a parameter in which to establish his location and fulfil his purpose on earth. He expected Abraham to create something out of what he saw and make something out of it. The result of his walking in that direction after seeing was his testimony given by his servant in Genesis 24:35-36. Abraham was able to walk through the land while seeing and creating what he saw as intangible things that he was able to transform into tangible things-into Camels, donkeys, silver and gold and servants. Remember that Abraham himself was an employer. This can be seen when he went to rescue Lot with 318 men brought up in his house (Gensis14:14). This can't be a description of an employee but an employer. Abraham was not just an employer but a trainer of an army. That is why he was called a Prince. He was a powerful man of faith because of his faith in God and his material wealth.

THE LAW OF PLACE- ISAAC POSITIONED HIMSELF IN THE RIGHT PLACE AS AN EMPLOYER

As we have already established, the place or the location or the position in which you are has an effect on the results you produce ultimately. We see the law of place at work in the life of Isaac. Isaac positioned himself by taking God's word not to run away from famine by going to Egypt but facing the challenges of famine while exploiting the resources in the land of the philistines to make him rich. Isaac was in the right place, at the right time and doing the right thing. Despite the famine which is mainly created by drought, Isaac went into irrigation by taking advantage of underground water. He positioned himself, as someone has put, as a commercial farmer who took advantage of the economic crisis in that place where he was and produced a crop to meet that need. The result was a turnaround. He had sown in that land and this was the point of his turn around.

The Bible in Genesis26:12 says that Isaac became rich and his wealth grew as a result of being in the right place. He was an employer with servants whom we now call employees. The right place is the place that God has designed for you to be in for Him to bless you. It seems each one of us has something to do, a place to be in, a time when to act to bring a turnaround in our lives. What is your right place, what is your right time and what is the right seed for you to sow-to invest?

THE LAW OF PLACE -THREE PERCENT OF THE WORLD'S POPULATION GETTING NINETY-SEVEN PERCERNT OF THE WORLD'S SHARE OF WEALTH

According to Bob Proctor he says that research has established that 3 percent of the world's population get 97 percent of the world's wealth and vice versa. I have depicted this in the diagram below:

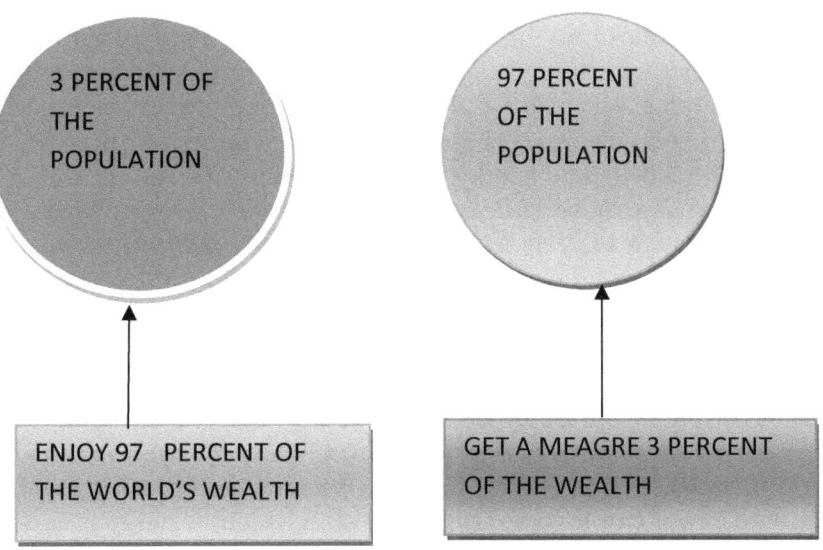

FIGURE 2: THE DISTRIBUTION OF THE WORLD'S WEALTH

According to Proctor, the result is that the 97 percent of the world's population depend on the 3 percent of the world's population. The 3 percent in a way control the majority using their wealth which in turn makes them have power to control the resource allocation and protect their wealth. One of the explanations is that those within the 3 percent are employers. They have chosen the risky side and when things go well for them they end up enjoying the result of their risk taking.

Where do you desire to be paid from? Do you desire to be paid from the 3 percent of the world's wealth or from the 97 percent? The choice you make on which side to be paid whether as an employer or employee matters. The choice you make either to be an employee or an employer can make a difference. *If you decide to be an employer, you embark on a journey to moving from the majority who get less to the minority in society who get more. In short you transit from being among the poor to being among the rich in society.*

THE LAW OF PLACE - THE MAJORITY ARE PLACED ON THE EASY SIDE THAT IS WHY THEY ARE PAID LESS AND ARE POOR

You need to have an understanding that having a business undertaking or being an employer is not easy sailing. You meet storms as you sail across the ocean called business before you reach your final harbour/port.

Understanding will help you realize that the majority of us want to take the easy side. Like some workmates told me as I shared with them some of these ideas that they would rather be employees because they were assured a pay, many think like this. Another said she would rather be an employee and an employer at the same time because it was more secure. You can see the power of the mind in bringing such understanding. *Since the majority are on the side of those who think like these colleagues of mine with an employee mentality, they end up leaving the few with an employer mentality who end up enjoying the fruit of being employers.*

We need to have an understanding of the benefits of being employers despite it not being an easy route to take. I have so far demonstrated in this writing the beauty of being your own boss. *Those of us who have experienced the agony that we have experienced as employees and understood these dynamics wish we could start life all over.* If this was to happen, we would from the very beginning venture into being employers. This is the side which is sweeter for you and me. As the man of God Myles Munroe put it, many people find themselves in jobs they do not like. They work simply for a pay check and as such waste their potential as a result. It pays for us to invest ourselves in that which will give us fulfilment when we choose to be employers.

CHAPTER 3: THE EMPLOYER IN YOU

WHAT IS YOUR KIND? AN EMPLOYEE OR AN EMPLOYER?

What is your kind? Are you born an employee or an employer? I have come to believe that you were born an employer. You have an employer kind in you even when you find yourself with an employee mind. In God's creation, He was able to create unique species. Vegetation produces according to its kind. An orange tree produces oranges as its fruit, a tomato plant produces a tomato as its fruit. Even for us all human beings, each one of us has our own kind. I am now fully convinced that I am a unique specie. You and I were created in the image and likeness of God. This means that we, like God, have the ability to create and to make. You are such a kind of person who can design and build things.

While an orange plant, as it brings forth its fruit, has no innovative ability to invent things, you and I are a different kind that has the ability to invent and innovate products and services. Someone has said King David was able to invent music that is in the psalms as he looked into himself. One time I told someone that I was an engineer, not an academic engineer but a self-made engineer with the ability to design and make things. I am then able to bring order to my created products and services ready for consumption by the consumers. *You as God's masterpiece, were wired with potential and were blessed and commanded to:*

(1) Be fruitful

(2) multiply

(3) fill the earth (distribution)

(4) subdue to the extent that you ultimately dominate.

Do you see an employer already embedded in you from creation?

WORKING DEFINITIONS OF EMPLOYER AND EMPLOYEE

The two words employer and employee are derived from the word employ. What then comes into your mind and mine is that there is an aspect of employing something for both the employer and the employee. Both own something that is being employed to produce a product or service. To employ is to put something into action with the view of producing a product or service for the market.

DEFINITION OF TERMS EMPLOY, EMPLOYEE AND EMPLOYER

The words employ, employee and employer have been defined below to guide our discussion. On the word employ one of the synonyms for it is work and engagement. As pointed out above, the words *employ/ee* and *employ/er* are derived from the word employ. **While both the employee and employer are employing their expertise, it is their work relations, what they put in and what they get from employing their expertise that differs.** What the employee owns, that is his or her knowledge, skills, intelligence, experience, time and other aspects as human capital are converted into labour and sold to the employer to get a wage or salary. The employer employs his or her knowledge, skills, intelligence, time and capital which are invested together with labour inputs in order to realize dividends or interest. **The employer purchases and owns the means of production which includes owning the employee, capital and entrepreneurial skills.**

WHO AN EMPLOYER IS AND WHO AN EMPLOYEE IS

So who is an employer and who is an employee? The employee is one who sells his or her labour for a wage or a salary. In other words, an employee is one who employs his or her resources in order to be paid a wage or salary in return. An employer is one who sells his efforts for a dividend or interest as a return to one's investment. In this regard, the employer employs his or her resources in order to have returns to his employment in terms of dividends. **The difference between the two is in perspectives. Their thinking is different.** They are in a master-servant relationship. Further **the difference between the two is in the payment or rewards they get as a result of the positioning they take resulting from the perspectives they have about themselves.**

The perspective they have about themselves determines the extent to which each of them end up going or becoming. The perspective also results in the position each of them ends up taking in a given organization or set up.

The other difference is in the ownership of the resources. The employer owns the employee, the capital and the land plus the entrepreneur skills while the employee does not own the employer. **What the employee owns in terms of skills including time is sold in exchange for a wage or salary.** The employer pays the employee the wage or salary and him or her as an employer who owns the means of production gets the dividends from the proceeds of the enterprise.

What the employee depends on is only what is in the conditions of service. Beyond that the employee has no further claim. Assuming he/she collapsed dead and left a family behind, all the employer will do is to give the employee's family the benefits according to what was agreed upon in the conditions. The employer will not say that the family be given shares in the company for the huge contribution he or she made to the organization.

The employee depends on his or her employer for survival while the employer depends on the company employees making profits for him. *Comparatively, the employer becomes richer than the employee based on the decisions they made at the very beginning.* The decision that each one makes regarding the potential in himself or herself and how one exploits it makes a difference in the output we get.

What is worth noting when we look at both the employee and the employer is that they both offer 'labour', knowledge, skills and experience towards the production of a product or service. *The main difference is that the employer adds capital to the equation and assumes ownership. It is ownership that determines what each one of them will reap at the end of the day.*

THE LAW OF SOWING AND REAPING AT WORK AS REGARDS BEING AN EMPLOYEE AND AN EMPLOYER.

Remember, a man reaps what he sows. If you sow labour, you will reap a wage or a salary. If you sow capital, land, entrepreneurship plus labour which may be your own or hired, you will reap profits which will result in dividends. Of course there is a risk of reaping losses. While the employee looks for favour from the employer, the employer looks for loyalty and commitment from the employee. The employer is a "self-made person."

THE EMPLOYER'S MAIN INTEREST IS HIMSELF OR HERSELF

Clearly you see that despite Laban appreciating Jacob to have been a major contributor to his wealth increase, he had no intentions for Jacob to share in the wealth. *It took Jacob's shrewdness to have made a turnaround in his life.* Luke16:1-11 talks about a shrewd manager who was commended by his master for being shrewd. For Jacob as a shrewd manager, waiting for Uncle Laban to improve his conditions of service was going to leave him in the same state-working hard but simply for sustenance. Uncle Laban's main interest was mainly in enriching himself. Whatever interest he may had for the employee, Jacob, was to the extent that he was pursuing his business interest. *This principle of pursuing self-interest is at work in the employee-employer relationship.*

THE MASTER VERSUS THE SERVANT BUSINESS RELATIONSHIP – THE EMPLOYER VERSUS EMPLOYEE RELATIONSHIP

As we have already established, the master, the employer, is the owner of the means of production. He/she owns the source of survival for a servant-the employee. The master uses authority to get what he/she wants from the employee, the servant. He/she can even give illogical instructions to the servant and the servant who is afraid of losing his or her job complies. *While the master uses authority, the employer uses loyalty to get a livelihood from the master through the pay-the salary or wage.*

THE "ABUSE" OF AN EMPLOYEE BY THE EMPLOYER

When you carefully consider what Jacob was telling Uncle Laban, his employer, how he had fared with him as his employer, we see that Jacob was in a way telling Uncle Laban that he had abused him for the many years he had worked for him. **Despite his managerial skills and business acumen coupled with all the contributions he had made, he was paid peanuts (Genesis30: 27-30).** Although Laban knew what he benefited from Jacob given the difference he brought to his business, he in turn gave him peanuts. *Had Jacob not repositioned himself, Laban would have continued abusing him.*

AN EMPLOYEE AS AN UNDERVALUED "EMPLOYER"

The employee was born an employer as far as God created Him/ her. But he/she undervalued himself/herself to the level of being an employee since this is the easier route to take. Despite what he/she has in terms of potential to be an employer, as an employee he /she is valued to the level that the employer is able to pay him or her. *By taking up the position of an employee, who should have been an employer, he/she ends up being paid from the cost of production not from dividends.*

THE WORTH OF AN EMPLOYEE IS MAINLY DETERMINED BY THE EMPLOYER THROUGH THE PAYCHECK

Since you are a seller of labour as an employee your worth is basically determined by your employer. He or she has to decide how much he or she is capable of paying you not how much you may really be worth being paid. *The rule is that the supplier of labour gets less than the supplier of capital. Since the majority of people take the supply of labour in the supply chain, the returns on the labour supply is generally lower than the returns on the supply of capital.* The supply of labour gets wages or salaries and the supply of capital gets a dividend or interest depending on the level of the capital supply.

THE EMPLOYER'S OBJECTIVE IN HIS OR HER MIND IS NOT TO MAKE YOU RICH BUT TO MAKE HIMSELF OR HERSELF RICH

The objective of the employer is not for making the employee rich but himself or herself. He or she thinks about acquiring wealth for himself or herself and does not look at the employee becoming rich. When you look at Laban and Jacob in Genesis 30:31-35, we see that while Jacob had intentions to become rich, Laban did not want him to progress. When a very brilliant suggestion was brought by Jacob of getting the colours he wanted to make him start building up his wealth, Laban agreed to the idea. However, those are the very colours which Laban removed and gave to his children to tend away from Jacob.

THE BEAUTY ABOUT A MASTER (AN EMPLOYER) -IT PAYS TO BE A MASTER

Now let us look at the beauty of being a master or an employer as opposed to being an employee. *The employer has more independence in terms of the use of his/her time, potential, knowledge and skills.* For me as an employee I have to make sure I go to bed early so that I wake up to report for work at the stipulated time. I go at the stipulated time to avoid reporting late. For an employer, he/she can go to bed when he/she deems fit to do so. He or she can be on his/her bed issuing instructions to employees by phone or email or any other means like skype. Thank God for technology like the use of phones and internet solutions.

The master can be as tired just as the servant but the master will sit at the table and tell the servant to serve him (Luke17:7-9).The servant may serve the master without the master being obliged to say thank you. Even if he says thank you to the servant the master is not mandated. A thank you to the servant would otherwise be a bonus to the employee.

FREEDOM IS THE BEST REWARD FOR YOUR WORK

According to www.fox news.com/us/2015/06/03/10 truths that sustain successful entrepreneurs, *there are many people who make million dollars a year, but are slaves to a job or boss they do not respect. The best earnings from your work as an entrepreneur is the freedom to do what you want and get the most out of your life.* This is the best for an entrepreneur having freedom. The entrepreneur has the freedom to know when to wake up on a particular day. He/she may decide to do business while in the bedroom especially with the current technology. To the contrary, the employee sacrifices his/her freedom to the employer/entrepreneur for security and some level of certainty in his/her salary. He has to submit to the instructions of the employer even when they may not make sense to him or her.

AN EMPLOYER AS AN INVESTOR AND AN EMPLOYEE AS A TAKER

Dr. John Edmund Haggai in his Book the Influential Leader says that there are two kinds of people in the world: the investors and the takers. According to him *investors see 'potent' in the potential and capitalize on it. By contrast, the takers do not see giving as an investment and try to hoard whatever they have.* Ultimately, the investors win and the takers do not. Of course he is referring to those who give as investors and those who receive as takers.

In connection with our discussion on employers and employees, I relate employers to investors and employees to takers. They both employ some investment but the employee in contrast to the employer only employs his or her labour to receive a salary or a wage. He or she is a taker. *The investor gives out his or her capital into a business venture expecting returns to his or her investment.* He/she sees potency in potential and capitalize on it. Eccliastes11:1 says cast your bread upon the waters and after sometime you will find it. Dr. Haggai's friend has been quoted in his Book the Influential Leader as having said that when you cast your bread upon the waters after sometime you will find it-toasted. *Applying this to employers, they in a way cast their capital on water and after sometime they find it-toasted.*

To the contrary, employees (the takers) see investment as a hard thing to venture into and as something that takes long to give back the returns to investment. Hence they opt for what is easier and faster which is becoming an employee. What we can see as the difference between the two categories is in the way they see things in their minds. Very few people see what employers see. The majority see an employee in themselves. This then explains why the majority of people are employees (takers) and few are employers (investors).

WHERE ARE YOU PAID FROM? ARE YOU PAID FROM COST OR FROM DIVIDENDS

You as an employee are a cost to the organization. To understand this you need to ask yourself: Am I paid from cost of production or from profits? If you have never thought through, take note that *your payment is part of the cost of production for the organization you work for.* Remember that the goal for an employer is to minimize costs in order to maximize returns to investment. ***Since you supply labour to the organization, you are part of the target for cost minimization by the organization.*** This explains why you may not be paid according to the actual value that you add to the organization.

The employer on the other hand is paid from profits after they are declared as dividends. This is where it matters most. ***The motive for an employer is to minimize costs and maximize shareholders value.*** In so doing you as an employee will end up being underpaid in relation to what you would have got if you had placed yourself on the employer side. From which side would you love to be paid? Where are you currently being paid from? Are you comfortable with this situation? What decisions are you going to take regarding your future with respect to what you get from the value you add to the organization you work for? ***Remember, the difference starts at whether you are the owner or not.***

ARE YOU SELLING YOUR TIME AND BRAINS FOR A SALARY OR FOR DIVIDEND?

The workplace is designed for you and me to spend those hours for the employer *if you are an employee.* What this means is that ***as an employee most of your thinking is for the employer's interest than for yourself.*** You spend most of the time thinking how to bring out the products or services that the employer wants in exchange for a wage. In a way, ***your mind got sold up to the employer just as your time had been sold to him/her when you entered into an employment contract.*** Had you not entered into an employment contract, you were going to have a bigger percentage of your time in your control as an employer. This is why as an employee you have conditions of service. They stipulate how your time is used as an employee. A bigger percentage is sold to the employer. ***But if you became an employer, it would mean that thinking for yourself was going to be allocated almost hundred percent of your time. I believe that it is at this point that the difference in wealth acquisition starts.***

THE IMPORTANCE OF VALUE IN THE EMPLOYMENT MARKET

For each one of us, there is some value placed on us in the eyes of some people and in our own eyes. The value people put on us determines how they treat us and what they pay us for it. In addition, the value we place on ourselves determines how we interact with the world around us. If the value you place on yourself equals the value people place on you, you accept what they label you. If you place a lower value on yourself than the value people place on you, you will reject rewards from such since they are beyond your expectation. Accepting their label on you may result in you reaching a level of incompetence where you end up failing to perform to people's expectation. Now *if the value you place on yourself is higher than the value people place on you, you reject what they offer you since your expectation is higher than the label placed on you.* This can be called self-promotion. Remember that you are a carrier of value and as such you are value positive. *As regards employment an employee places his or her value on himself or herself equivalent to that placed on him/her by the employer.* There is a value that an employee puts on himself or herself. This is the value which equates with the value the employer places on the employee. This value is translated into a wage or a salary. The value of the employee in the eyes of an employer is to the extent that the employee adds value to make products or services for the employer to have profit. The value of the employer in the eyes of an employee is to the extent that the employee depends on the employer for his or her livelihood. Naturally the employee puts higher value on the employer than the employer puts on the employee.

The moment one realizes that the value on himself/ herself is higher than that placed on him/her, the person has higher chances of rejecting the offer by an employer. *It is those who put higher value on themselves in the employment market who end up being employers. Employers place a higher value on themselves in their own eyes. They realize that they have too high value to be equated to the salary or the wage.* Again it is the issue of the mind since *value is established in the mind.* The value created in one's mind makes a difference in the decisions an employee or an employer makes in the work undertakings and this is what determines the rewards each of them receives from the other. *Value is key in this matter. The value you place on yourself is key since you can either value yourself as an employee or as an employer and that determines what you ultimately reap.* According to Proverbs18:16, it is your gift (your value) that makes people place high value on you. For you to come into the presence of great men or women there must be something in you that you bring into their presence. There are two elements that can be brought in the presence of great men or women. *You either bring your gift into the presence of great men or women as an employee working for them or as an employer exchanging ideas with them that may lead to them making decisions such as you becoming a shareholder in their business undertakings.*

THE CONTRIBUTION OF AN EMPLOYEE AND THAT OF AN EMPLOYER IN A BUSINESS UNDERTAKING

All things being equal, the employee gives the employer more than what the employer gives the employee in relation to what each puts in regarding labour. Of course, *the employer took a risk to invest his or her capital into the business enterprise and the employee only came to offer his or her labour to the employer.* All that the employer sees in the employee is labour and how the labour translates into products or services and hence profitability. This is supplied in form of energy, knowledge, skills and experience that the employee brings into the organization to transform the capital investments into wealth for the employer. The employee sees his livelihood in the employer. *The employer determines the worth of the employee in terms of the employee being able to get a wage for his or her living. You are paid to the extent that you have valued yourself equivalent to the value the employer places on you.* It is this that makes the employee try to put in all his/her mind and effort to please the employer lest he/ she is fired. The master can continue keeping you as long as he/ she is convinced that you are able to continue putting in your best into the business with at least some minimal increment in your pay which entices you to stay on.

LABAN THE EMPLOYER'S VALUATION OF HIS COMPANY AND THE VALUE PLACED ON JACOB AS AN EMPLOYEE

After being given the manifesto by Jacob that he wanted to leave Laban's company, we see that Laban agreed with Jacob's presentation of the facts at hand. This can be seen in his reaction to Jacob. In Genesis 30: 31, Laban asked Jacob what he wanted to be given to him for his wages. The question is: What was he giving him before this time? Laban should have agreed with Jacob that he was giving him peanuts. *This is so because Laban undervalued Jacob's worth for many years and that Jacob never confronted Laban.*

Now that Jacob had valued himself highly, Laban was willing to go higher in his payment in order to keep Jacob in his company. It was at this point of valuing himself highly that Jacob had a turnaround to benefit from his managerial skills and his story changed. The result was that he finally became an employer like Laban. The same can happen to you and me if we reposition our minds by putting higher value than what employers can place on us.

THE VALUE OF AN EMPLOYEE IN THE EYES OF THE EMPLOYER AND THE VALUE OF AN EMPLOYEE IN HIS OR HER OWN EYES

For each one of us, there is some value placed on us in the eyes of some people and in our own eyes. The value people put on us determines how they treat us and what they pay us for it. In addition, the value we place on ourselves determines how we interact with the world around us. For the employer/employee relationship, there is value in the eyes of an employer regarding an employee and the employee regarding his or her own value. There is a value that an employee puts on himself or herself. The value of the employee in the eyes of an employer is to the extent that it is the employee who makes products or services for the employer to have profit. The value of the employer in the eyes of an employee is to the extent that the employee depends on the employer for his or her livelihood. Naturally the employee puts higher value on the employer than the employer puts on the employee. This makes a difference in what each of them receives from the other.

All things being equal, the employee gives the employer more than what the employer gives the employee in relation to what each puts in regarding labour. Of course, the employer took a risk to invest his or her capital into the business enterprise and the employee only came to offer his or her labour to the employer. All that the employer sees in the employee is labour and how the labour translates into products or services. This is supplied in form of energy, knowledge, skills and experience that the employee brings into the organization to transform the capital investments into wealth for the employer. The employee sees his livelihood in the employer. The employer determines the worth of the employee in terms of the employee being able to get a wage for his or her living. It is this that makes the employee try to put in all his mind and effort to please the employer lest he or she is fired. The master can continue keeping you as long as he or she is convinced that you are able to continue putting in your best into the business with at least some minimal increment in your pay which entices you to stay on.

Value is key in this matter. *The value you place on yourself is key since you can either value yourself as an employee or as an employer and that determines what you ultimately reap.* According to Proverbs18:16, it is your gift (your value) that makes people place high value on you. For you to come into the presence of great men or women there must be something in you that you bring into their presence. There are two elements that can be brought in the presence of great men or women. *You either bring your gift into the presence of great men or women as an employee working for them or as an employer exchanging ideas with them that may lead to them making decisions such as you becoming a shareholder in their business undertakings.*

LABAN AS THE EMPLOYER'S VALUATION OF HIS COMPANY AND THE VALUE PLACED ON JACOB AS AN EMPLOYEE

After being given the manifesto by Jacob that he wanted to leave Laban's company, we see that Laban agreed with Jacob's presentation of the facts at hand. This can be seen in his reaction to Jacob. In Genesis 30; 31, we are told that Laban asked Jacob what he wanted to be given to him for his wages. The question is: What was he giving him before this time? Laban should have agreed with Jacob that he was giving him peanuts. This is so because you can see it from his response when Jacob confronted him. He should have undervalued his worth for many years even though Jacob never confronted him.

Now that Jacob had valued himself highly, Laban was willing to go higher in his payment in order to keep Jacob in his company. It was at this point of valuing himself highly that Jacob had a turn around to benefit from his managerial skills and his story changed. The result was that he finally became an employer like Laban. This is what can happen to you if you repositioned yourself. *Remember, You are paid to the extent that you have valued yourself equivalent to the value the employer places on you.*

JACOB'S VALUATION OF HIMSELF

While in Laban's company and having worked for many years, Jacob could have been deceived to think that he was doing fine as an employee. It was not until when he started thinking about his hard work in connection with his gains that he made a decision to reposition himself. First Jacob saw himself as having proved to be a good manager over Laban's estate. He told Laban to let him go back to his home country, for Laban knew his service which he had done for him (Genesis 30:28-30). *You need to realize your value.*

Jacob undertook an evaluation of the first part of his years of stay with Laban for over fourteen and the service he gave to Laban. He saw how much those years had brought to Laban. He saw himself having gained experience by being a good manager. He thought through and came back to his senses that assuming he used the over fourteen years on his own estates, what God did to bless Laban because of him Jacob would have been his. *The difference between the employer (the owner) and employee is that the employer owns the means of production while the employee owns skills.* Ultimately those who own capital as a means of production derive equity from the profits while those who provide labour as a means of production earn wages.

He should have learned that in this life we have a choice either to own capital or labour. In the over fourteen years he worked for Laban, Jacob had a choice either to own capital or to provide labour. He should have got insights that Labourers or employees throughout history get a small fraction of the labour costs from a company. Actually in the books of account, labour costs are removed before profits are declared since ***Profit = Revenue – Cost. This means that the owners of capital are the owners of profit.*** An employee is then a cost of production (a liability) in the books of accounts since the wages he gets are a cost to the organization. He or she is only an asset when it comes to his or her contribution to the organization in terms of adding value to the means of production. But when it comes to the employer's cost of production, an employee is a cost to the organization. That is why *employers aim to minimize costs in order to maximize their returns*. One of the costs they try to minimize is labour cost which is what goes to the employees.

After placing a higher value on himself, something started working in Jacob's mind. He should have concluded that apart from him undervaluing himself to have accepted Laban's conditions, the employer, uncle Laban, had also undervalued him. *His worth was higher than what he placed on himself and was placed on him by Laban in form of the wages he was getting*. This realization is which brought a turnaround in Jacob finally becoming an employer.

LABAN'S VALUATIONS OF JACOB

In the eyes of Laban, Jacob was an "asset" to him in as far as growth to his business was but a "liability" or a "cost" in as far as remuneration was concerned. Despite what Jacob had put in the organization, Laban mistreated him to the extent that he kept on changing his wages ten times (Genesis31:6-7). *Laban mistreated Jacob despite the value he brought into his business.* He was trying to minimize costs of labour in order to maximize on his returns. This he managed to do for some years until Jacob came to realization that this was not the best for him.

THE STATUS FOR JACOB AND THAT OF LABAN BEFORE GENESIS30:25

As you read the conversation between Jacob and Laban in Genesis30:25-34, you see what was there for Jacob and for Laban which made a difference in their status in society. *Jacob put up his case of hard work, faithfulness as a servant and his good management.* Despite his argument which was valid, the result was simply being rewarded with wages by Laban. *Laban on the other hand knew what Jacob was carrying in terms of capabilities to grow his business.* Laban saw the turnaround in his business from the time Jacob got involved. Instead of rewarding him accordingly, *he only gave Jacob wages which on principle do not grow the way dividends grow*. The following is what made a difference between the two before Jacob repositioned himself:

JACOB'S STATUS

- Jacob was an employee working for Laban
- He was a wise man but poor man.

- He had good managerial skills
- He was a faithful manager
- He was carrying a blessing from God through his grandfather Abraham and his father Isaac.
- God was with Jacob
- He was giving tithe to God from his wages as he had vowed earlier in Genesis28:20-22 and confirmed in Genesis31:13 years later by God Himself.
- ***His reward despite what he was carrying and all what he did to Laban's enterprise were wages.***
- ***He was poor despite being a wise man full of faith in God.***

LABAN'S STATUS

- He was an employer as the owner of the business
- He as an employer owned Jacob's brains, knowledge, skills, talents and time
- He was an idol worshipper. He was a heathen.
- Being an idol worshipper, there is a possibility that he was not giving tithe to God.
- He benefited from the wisdom, capabilities and the management skills of Jacob and God's blessings on Jacob.
- ***His rewards were dividends.***
- ***His wealth grew and he became wealthier than he was before Jacob started working for him.***
- ***He was a wise rich man.***

Having illustrated some of the contrasts between Jacob and Laban, we see that ***Jacob's outcome was poverty because of the position he played as an employee in the midst of wealthy. The laws of position(place) and ownership were at work.*** On the other hand, the outcome for Laban was wealthy because even for him the laws of position (place) and ownership were at work. ***He was in a position of an employer while Jacob was in the position of an employee.*** The employee owns only labour while the employer buys the labour and makes it his or hers. The employer also owns the idea, capital and land. The outcome is predictable. You do not need to know rocket science in order for you to predict the outcome of the two. *The place in which you position yourself as regards ownership determines the outcomes you get from the position and the ownership.*

What is your outcome now? Why are you where you are now? Where do you want to be going forward? Do you want to be like Jacob or Laban as regards wealthy before Genesis30:25-31? *Your outcome is predictable depending on the position you are occupying now or you will occupy going forward.*

THE BAD SIDE OF UNCLE LABAN (THE EMPLOYER) WORKED OUT TO BECOME JACOB'S GOOD

For Jacob, we see that the toughness of Laban on him worked out for his good. *The toughness of Laban helped him to bring out the employer in him.* Laban's unfair treatment of Jacob made Jacob to be uneasy and forced him to reposition himself into becoming an employer. As a man carrying the blessing of Abraham and Isaac on him, *the negatives he encountered from Laban were an opportunity for him to bring out the best out of himself.* Manna may stop dropping from heaven for a purpose. And ravens may stop bringing you food and the brook from which water was coming may dry up for a purpose. As the Bible tells us in Romans8:28, to those who love God and are called for His purpose, all things work together for good. *For Jacob trials produced the employer in him. What in his life happened before Genesis30:25 was the springboard for the results that he ended up producing in Genesis30:43.* All things worked out for good for Jacob.

THE GOOD SIDE OF UNCLE LABAN

To make sure that we do not only concentrate on the bad side of Uncle Laban as an employer, we have to look at the good side of him as pointed out below;

- He took care of Jacob who only went to him with a staff in his hand. His home was a refuge for Jacob for a start. Jacob, a fugitive, running away from a brother found a place to stay and work from.

- *He was a business minded person.* As such Laban was the right person for Jacob to have associated with at his early life.

- *He was a facilitator and the source of wealth* that Jacob acquired.

- *Uncle Laban should have been a great thinker.* He knew how to maximize the utilization of Jacob as a resource so that he could give him the best of himself and, in turn, pay him a wage. He was able to pay less in return for higher value. *Laban actually knew why he should think and came up with an idea to invest and ended up taking care of Jacob who only knew how to think.*

- Uncle *Laban was able to employ a man with very good managerial skills even when he himself could not have had such skills* and was able to give him a wage for it.

- *He knew the importance of belonging where fewer people are found* (being among the employers who are fewer compared to employees who are in the majority). *He chose to be on the side of employers as opposed to being on the side of employees.* Jacob had chosen at first to be on the side of the majority-employees, until he refused to be conformed to the pattern of this world and mind renewal took place in him that resulted in him experiencing transformation into being a shareholder in Laban's business.

- Uncle Laban already had a base-a source of Jacob's wealth. *Your wealth could be with an uncle Laban somewhere, you can get it from him as long as you reposition yourself in the mind.*

- *Laban was the one from whom Jacob leveraged on to acquire the wealth he ultimately got.* So Jacob's history of being an employee and later an employer cannot be complete without mentioning Laban. Laban was a great entrepreneur despite having weaknesses.

BEING AN EMPLOYEE OR AN EMPLOYER IS A CHOICE YOU MAKE

Being an employer or an employee then is a choice that you make. You either decide to be a master (an employer) to someone or a servant (an employee) to someone. God told man to behold what He had given him- plants with seed in them (Genesis1:29-30) and God told man to manage what he had given him (Genesis2:15). God gave man business to do on the onset. Each one of us has some business to do whether we are doing it or not. *God put man in the position of an employer.* We see it from Adam to Noah. We also see it in Abraham and Isaac. These were employers. Of course they employed servants who were in a sense employees.

DID JACOB MAKE A CHOICE TO BECOME AN EMPLOYEE?

All along I used to think that Jacob found himself working for his uncle through circumstances beyond his control. This is not really true. *Jacob made a choice on which side to take. I came to realize this when I asked a question what if he put the conditions he gave Jacob later about sharing the proceeds from the onset? Wouldn't he have been a shareholder from the beginning?* You may say may be *Laban* would have refused because he had not known what Jacob could do. But the question is: Did Jacob have the concept of shareholding in mind from the very beginning? Did he ever try to make a proposal to Laban? We are not told but one could see that, as is the case for many of us, **Jacob chose the easier option-Becoming an employee.**

JACOB CAME BACK TO HIS SENSES

Like the prodigal seen in Luke 15 Jacob might have recalled his grandfather's Abraham's wealth (Genesis24:1, 35). He might have also recalled his own father Isaac's wealth (Genesis26:12-13). **He looked at his status for over 14 years that as normal until when his thinking changed.** He then came up with the option to leave and go back to his father's home. I believe Jacob could have already developed some ideas of how he could own his own enterprise. I see it in the way he reacted to Laban and made the proposal immediately Laban told him name your wages. **Jacob had at this point come to his senses that it pays to be a shareholder.**

TURNAROUND IN JACOB'S STATUS

It was not until when Jacob's thinking like an employee changed to thinking like an employer (like Laban) did he see God's purpose regarding his wellbeing getting fulfilled in his life. The verse Genesis 30:43 only became a reality when Jacob repositioned himself. The verse says that thus the man became exceedingly prosperous and had large flocks, female and male servants and Carmel's and donkeys. What we see in this verse regarding Jacob *that resulted from repositioning himself* is that:

- The man become exceedingly prosperous.
- His prosperity was seen in him having
    - (i)   large flocks
    - (ii) female and male servants (employees)
    - (iii) Carmel's and donkeys (transport facilities).

JACOB'S SECRET FOR HIS TURNAROUND

The question is: How did this become true for Jacob? The answer is simple:

- Jacob's turnaround is in Genesis 30:25-26. It came when He said to Laban that he needed to be released to go to his father's homeland.

- *Jacob repositioned himself in his mind as an employer.*
- *He created something in his mind which led to him making wealth.* His turnaround was when he stopped thinking and acting like an employee of Laban to thinking that he also had the ability to be like uncle Laban –that he needed to apply the business acumen that he possessed for years.
- *He moved further from just working hard for Laban to making profit by becoming an employer*-by owning some female and male servants making money for him.

WHEN DID THE TURNAROUND COME ABOUT IN JACOB'S MIND?

The turnaround came when Jacob said to Laban:

- Send me away-retire me
- Retire me so that I can go to my own place and to my country.
- Give me my resources that I have acquired while working for you.
- For you know the services I have done for you.

REALIZING THAT IT IS NOT ABOUT WORKING OR NOT WORKING TO EXPECTATION AND MAKING A DECISION TO DO THINGS DIFFERENTLY

The question is: How did this become true for Jacob to have become rich? The answer is simple: Jacob repositioned himself in his mind as an employer. *He created something in his mind which led to him making wealth. His turnaround was when he stopped thinking and acting like an employee of Laban to thinking that he also had the ability to be like uncle Laban*. He realized that he needed to apply the business acumen that he possessed for years. He moved further from just working hard for Laban to making profit for himself. This was to be seen in him becoming an employer-by owning some female and male servants making money for him. Jacob's turnaround is in Genesis 30:25-26. It came when Jacob repositioned himself.

DO YOU DESIRE TO SEE CHANGE? YOU MAY NEED TO CHANGE METHODOLOGY

According to Albert Einstein, he defined insanity as doing the same thing over and over again and expecting different results. *The same methodology gives you the same results if you do not change the methodology.* So if you do not change the way you do things, expect to get some results. *Your desire to see change will become a reality if only you change the way you do things.* You will need to break some patterns and have mind renewal that will result in transformation to make you prove the good, acceptable and perfect will of God (Romans12:2). *Jacob had not only to change the methodology but he had to change his way of thinking.*

ACKNOWLEDGING YOU ARE IN A WRONG POSITION OF AN EMPLOYEE

In order for social change to take place that will bring about transformation, you need to start by acknowledging that you are in a wrong place as an employee which explains why you depend on wages or a salary. *It is not until you conclude that being an employee is bad for you to change your position to that of an employer.*

JACOB USED HIS MIND TO IMAGINE AND BROUGHT ABOUT TRANSFORMATION

Jacob started by imagining in his mind owning assets as indicated in Genesis30:43 before he physically owned them. He first owned the intangible wealth in form of imagination before he had it in tangible form. It is this imagination that made him confront Laban and immediately an opportunity was given to him. He then jumped onto it and gave a business proposal to Laban about using colours to share in the wealth. Jacob's imagination: Getting the colours he wanted (Genesis 30:37-39) made a difference. In Genesis31:10-13 Jacob describes how it all happened. *It started with a dream from God and he picked it and acted upon it accordingly.*

THE SECRET WAS IN THE COLOUR RULE TO JACOB'S TURNAROUND

Each one of us could be having a secret towards bringing a turnaround in our economic status. We see that Jacob started with the dream in which he saw that the animals that mated gave three colours stripped, spotted and mottled. The Angel told Jacob to lift up his eyes and see that all the goats that mate with the flocks were stripped, spotted and mottled. God through the angel told Jacob the reason why He had intervened. He said that He had seen all that Laban was doing to him Jacob. *Jacob then implemented his dream and went into product development. The results of the power of imagination are recorded in Genesis 30:43.* It is Jacob's imagination that was combined with the dream revealed to him by God that led to his amassing wealth from Laban's enterprise. As already pointed out, *each one of us could be having a secret towards bringing a turnaround in our status.*

JACOB'S STRENGTH OF HIS DESIRE TO TRANSITION FROM EMPLOYEE TO EMPLOYER

"The size of your success is measured by the strength of your desire; the size of your dream; and how you handle disappointment along the way." Robert Kiyosaki.

Three things to be picked from the quote from Kayosaki:

1. The strength of your desire.

2. The size of your dream.

3. How you handle disappointment

As you read between the lines of Genesis 30:25-43, you see the three elements coming out. You can see the strength of Jacob's desire to make the value that was in him to pay off for him by the way he proposed the sharing formula between him and Laban. He suggested the use of colours. He used sticks to give him the colours that he wanted and he ended up becoming wealth.

JACOB'S SIZE OF HIS DREAM TO TRANSITION FROM EMPLOYEE TO EMPLOYER

I see Jacob dreaming big while in Laban's Enterprise. I see him dreaming owning camels, flocks, donkeys, male and female servants. I see him dreaming himself giving instructions to his workers. I see him making decisions regarding the wealth he would acquire in the near future. I see him dreaming getting out of Laban's Estate with wealth instead of just going out with wives and children as the only wealth. ***Dreams are key.*** The Bible says in Acts2:17-19 that young people shall see visions and old men shall dream dreams. No wonder we see Jacob dreaming about animals mating and him putting branches around where animals were mating to get the wealth he needed. ***Jacob's increase formula came out of a dream.***

JACOB'S HANDLING OF THE DISAPPOINTMENT AS HE TRANSITIONED FROM EMPLOYEE TO EMPLOYER

As you read Jacob's statement to Laban in Genesis30:25-30 and Genesis31:1-11, you see that Laban disappointed Jacob. Jacob expected Laban to treat him much better, but he got the opposite of his expectations. The secret for Jacob was on the handling of the disappointment. Actually he looked at the disappointment as a stepping stone to repositioning himself to become an employer. ***The disappointment could have made him get annoyed with*** *himself as to why he chose to be an employee. It instead made him to see the secret of ownership.*

WHAT AN EMPLOYEE GETS IS AS A RESULT OF THE SIDE WHICH HE OR SHE TAKES AS A POSITION

Experience has taught me that an employee may put in his best into the organization but that simply amounts to a wage or salary. At best the employee may get a bonus. The remuneration he or she gets at the end of the day is according to the side taken to become an employee at the very beginning. *Since the employee has taken the side of getting wages by investing labour, he or she reaps below the real value that he or she may put into the organization.* His or her rewards are in line with the position taken in the employee-employer relation. *Because he or she takes the position of an employee and sows labour, what is reaped are wages, fulfilling the law of sowing and reaping.* Since wages are part of costs, the issue with wages is that the employer aims to minimize costs in order to maximize his or her returns. The employee then ends up getting less than what he or she would have been paid under normal circumstances.

The employer who takes the position of ownership is in better a position, all things being equal. Whatever the employee generates is his or hers as the owner of the means of production which includes the employee as well. The employee may make whatever profits but clearly he or she knows that the profits are for the employer. *The many years spent working for the employer contributes to the accumulation of the employer's net worth in terms of wealth accumulation. So the employee is simply a 'tool' for wealth creation and ultimately wealth accumulation or acquisition for the employer.* Meanwhile the employee gets the wages or salary which is mainly for sustenance.

As already pointed out above and as we can so far see, the case in mind is that of Jacob who put in the best into Laban's enterprise but Laban in turn mistreated him and underpaid him. He changed his wages ten times (Genesis31:6-7). Jacob realized that he put in a lot but got less than what he should have got out of the effort he put in. *He could have realized that if what he put in was to be directed towards his personal investment, the returns would be higher than what he was getting from Laban. The law of investment with its multiplier effect could have come to Jacob's mind that the employer reaps proportionate to the investment he or she makes, provided the investment gets the expected returns.*

As one who takes the higher risk, he or she also reaps more than what an employee reaps. This was the experience that Jacob had with Laban. He wished he could get more but got less because he had put himself on the side where he only sold his labour. *The side you take matters as regards what you reap in the wealth creation and accumulation equation. You either get wages or dividends depending on which side you have positioned yourself.* The position you take in this employee-employer transaction makes the difference regarding what you reap at the end of the day. *So what is your position or what will be your position going forward?*

KNOWING WHEN TO LEAVE THE STAGE AS AN ACTOR

Interesting enough, humans have a tendency of continuing being on the stage acting even when it is apparent that they needed to leave. There is always a moment when you have to decide to put what you have in your mind into practice and this may require you leaving the stage where you are as an actor. If you have been acting as an employee, unless you switch roles while on the stage, you will continue acting as an employee. The rewards you will get will be those of an employee. *Jacob was on the stage as an employee and the rewards he got were those of an employee.* At a given point he thought of leaving the stage from which he acted as an employee and act as an employer. He had in his mind the need to leave Laban's business and go and start another pursuit outside Laban's spheres. When he approached Laban that he wanted to leave, Laban refused him to go because he was gaining from Jacob's contribution to his business.

Despite underpaying him as an employee, Laban knew Jacob's capabilities that contributed to the success of his business. *Jacob stayed around this time on different terms.* After achieving his objectives and having acquired the wealth from Laban, God told Jacob to leave because his time to be around Laban was over. *Thank God his wives told him to do whatever God was telling him to do.*

We need to learn here that in the place where we find ourselves, time and chance is given to us all (Ecclestiastes9:11). *It is therefore important for us to cease the opportunity and use it to our advantage. This is what an entrepreneur does. In life, we all have the same sunshine, the same seasons, the same twenty four hours a day but the difference is what each one of us does with the time and chance available to us.* In 1chronicles 12: 32 we are told about the children of Issachar who understood times and were able to move out of the place where they were with King Saul to go and join David. The good thing about them was that they understood times and knew what they were supposed to do. *We may be in the right place at the right time but we might be doing wrong things. Sometimes the things we are doing may not really be wrong but they may not be appropriate for us for a given time and the given understanding.* Understanding the time for the children of Issachar made them conclude that they were in the wrong place and doing the wrong thing. *They were to do the right thing if they had to change location– to repositioning themselves* to leave King Saul to join David.

For Jacob, Laban's place was the right place to go to at that time when he ran from his brother Esau because that is where he was to marry from so as to have children like Judah-the ancestor of Christ. So the right things he did for 14 years working for the two wives were done in the right place at the right time. *But after some years elapsed, timing made the right place to become a wrong place and therefore the right actions could no longer be done in Laban's company.*

We need to be in the right place at the right time and doing the right thing. Each of those variables namely place, time and thing (the idea) can be put in disequilibrium by one of them or by two of them and the other two get affected by the one or the two of them. For Jacob when he first went to be with Laban it was a right place for that time and he started doing the right thing working to get a wife. The thing he did was the same thing and the same seasons came his way. What changed in his mind was his perspective about what he was doing. *He started looking at Laban's place and working for Laban for wages as being a wrong idea. His outlook had changed with time.* Having reached this conclusion he attempted to leave but Laban restrained him from leaving. Given Laban's insistence that Jacob should not leave, Jacob used this opportunity as the right time to bargain for a shareholding deal with Laban. He managed to get what he was longing to get from Laban.

Imagine Jacob was all along in the right place for becoming rich but used the right time doing the 'wrong thing'. *When he did the 'the right thing' his status changed immediately-he became an employer.* He acquired the wealth he finally had because he did the right thing at the right time in the right place for that time even when it was a rough environment. However, afterwards the time for him to be with Laban had expired and he had to leave because Laban's countenance had changed and his children were up in arms against Jacob whom they thought had gotten their father's wealth. When Jacob realized it was wrong time to be in Laban's company, he decided to leave. In fact it is God who told him to leave and Jacob had to finally leave (Genesis 31:13).

If Jacob was going to continue being in Laban's company, the ending for him would have turned out to be a disaster because the timing was over. This is where many people like leaders make a mistake of holding on to the stage even when there timing is no more. In Genesis 31:13, God told Jacob to arise and get out of that land and return to the land of his family. *What we see here is that God does not just tell us to leave but also has timing when he tells us to leave.* In addition to telling us to leave, He also tells us to take an action by arising. "Now arise," God told Jacob. *When Jacob heard God telling him to leave, he arose and left.* Jacob did not behave like Lot in Sodom and Gomorrah who even when he was warned of danger and told to leave immediately took long to do so.

We need to realize that when God's timing comes for us to leave, He tells us to arise. God does not only tell us to arise when the hour has come but also gives us direction to take and the final destination to land. This is how safe we are under God's direction. No wonder David in Psalms23 acknowledged God as his shepherd and that he could not want-he would not be troubled. *The only thing needed here to clearly hear God say, "Now arise". The other thing required is to clearly get the direction in which to go.* Also required is to clearly get the place of the final destination when you hear him say arise.

For example, as can be seen in 2 Samuel from Chapter1 to chapter 9 the secret of David's success was inquiry from God. He inquired of God. "Should I go to defeat the Philistines?" "Should I leave this place where I am now since Saul has died and where exactly should I settle?" "Is it Hebron and which location in Hebron?" *The Bible says the steps of a righteous man are ordered by the Lord and he delights in his ways* (Psalms 37:23). For David, having his steps being ordered by the Lord meant quite a lot to him because everywhere he went God gave him success. We are told in 1Samuel 18:14 that in everything David did, he had great success because the LORD was with him. No wonder God said that He had found a man after His own heart and that he would do what He command him to do (Acts37:22).

The good element in the patriarchs including Jacob was that when they heard God speak they acted promptly. This is where many of us have missed it. When God tells us to do something we spend time debating about it and as such we miss the opportunities availed to us. This makes us not to change our status. I like the way the two beautiful wives of Jacob (beauty seen in the way they answered Jacob) answered Jacob in Genesis 31:16. They told to arise in the immediately and told him that whatever God has said to him, he was do it immediately by arising and leaving Laban. The two beautiful women told Jacob, "Now then, whatever God said to you, do." Many of us have just heard God speak but have not arisen and even when sometimes we might have arisen, we have not done what God told us to do. Sometimes even when we have done what God told us to do, we like Moses have done it wrongly (striking the rock twice). In some cases we have arisen but missed out on the timing to arise now and the time to do it.

We need to leave the current stage where we have been acting from and get into the unfamiliar territory when God has spoken to us. There is an eagle in each one of us requiring to fly if only we can decide to leave the stage from which we acted like chickens even when we are eagles. Someone has said "How can you be an eagle if you can't fly." *For an eaglet to start flying, it needs to leave the nest and move away from the familiar environment and venture into the unknown arena. This is where success lies for you and be like it turned out to be for Jacob.*

THE PRINCIPLES AND CHARACTERISTICS OF EMPLOYERS

Abraham the grandfather of Jacob had an employer mind. Isaac the father of Jacob had an employer mind. He was his own employer. He grew a crop and had a turnaround –a hundred fold of harvest. His wealth began to grow until he became very wealthy. The secret for Isaac was that he listened to God- about the place to be in and what to do in that place (Genesis26:1-12). The secret for these men was that they walked with God and that their faith was in God as a source of blessings.

To the contrary, Jacob found himself as an employee even when he was capable of being employer. He spent many years working for his uncle Laban. *As an employee, he worked under the principles that govern an employee.* These principles are enshrined in what are called conditions of service. These conditions of service have in them more of the protection of the interests of the employer than those of the employee. These conditions are designed to make the employee put in all his time and energy. Failure to which his job would come to an end.

Since Jacob was working under the principles that govern an employee, the results were those that are the result of the inputs from an employee. *The laws that govern an employee were at work in his life.* The employee laws have their limit beyond which they cannot perform otherwise. *To transform from being affected by employee laws to employer laws or principles, there was need for change in type of thinking and taking steps to make the new thoughts a reality.* For Jacob to be an employer, he needed to have certain principles that would enable him to have a breakthrough in his endeavours. There are principles which he learned from the two patriarchs Abraham and Isaac who were employers. For Abraham, he was an employer from the onset. His son Isaac followed suit by being an employer. They both had male and female servants whom we today call employees.

But *for Jacob something seems to have gone wrong in his mind.* This made him start from the other side of having employee principles. It took him many years to later reposition himself to having employer principles. It is this repositioning that made a difference in his life.

BEING IN THE RIGHT PLACE AT THE RIGHT TIME AND DOING THE RIGHT THING AS AN EMPLOYER

There is an adage that you are supposed to be in the right place at the right time doing the right thing. This is said to be a key thing in attaining success in our lives.

BALANCING THE THREE-RIGHT PLACE, RIGHT TIME AND RIGHT THING-THE SECRET FOR TURN AROUND TO SUCCESS

My observation of successful people both in the Bible and in the secular world is that what made them succeed in what they did was the a balance of the three variables;

1. Right place/placement
2. Right time/timing
3. Right thing(s)/ Right ideas

My insight into the three variables, place, time and thing (ideas) is that each of these variables can affect the outcome of our actions. For example Isaac in Genesis 26 wanted to leave Gerar (place) which according to timing was in famine and go to Egypt which seemed to be a right thing to him to do. Isaac thought Gerar was a wrong place so he had to move to go to the right place (Egypt) since it was the right time (time of famine) so that he would go and do right in Egypt (idea). *God intervened and told him that Gerar was the right place and the famine time was the right timing in which he was to do the right thing-planting seed.*

To Isaac, the place looked wrong, the timing looked wrong, the idea of growing a crop looked wrong. *However, when God told him that he was in a right place despite what he saw, he then looked at the famine time as the right time for him to grow a crop which was a good idea to do.* The result was a turnaround in his life. What we see is that place/placement can impinge on how we use time and the good ideas we have to give us some results. For some of us, we might be in the right place but are not or have not taken advantage of the time we have to implement the good ideas we have. Ecclesiastes 9:10-11 says that whatever your hands finds to do, do it with all your mighty within the place which you are and the timing that you have. Take advantage of the place where you are and the time which you have to plan, to acquire knowledge, to work hard and to invest.

OPERATING IN THE INTERSECTION OF THE RIGHT PLACE, RIGHT THING AND RIGHT TIME

As can be seen from the diagram below, there is a possibility that you are in the wrong place, doing the wrong thing at the wrong time. This is where you are existing but there is no essence for your existence. The other possibility is that you are in the right place at the wrong time and doing the wrong thing. Another possibility is that the time is right for you but you are in a wrong place and doing the wrong thing for your life. Yet another possibility is that you are doing a right thing but the place is wrong and the time is not right. Taking the thought further, some people are in the right place at the right time but they are doing the wrong thing. Others are in the right place and doing the right thing at the wrong time. There are also those who are doing the right thing at the right time but in a wrong place.

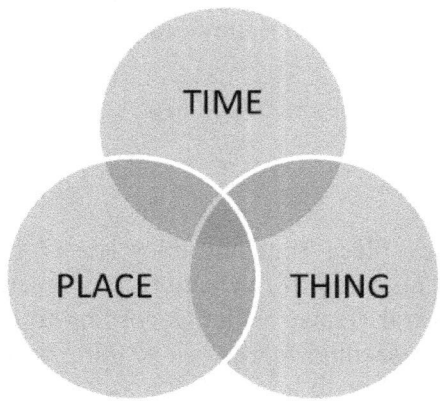

Figure 3 : THE INTERSECTION OF THE RIGHT PLACE, RIGHT TIME AND RIGHT THING

The best position for each one of us is the intersection of the three. As pointed out already, the saying goes that we need to be in the right place, at the right place doing the right thing. This is God's desire for you and me. This is the point where we derive satisfaction and fulfilment in life. Where are you operating from?

ABRAHAM'S PRINCIPLES AS ONE WHO HAD AN EMPLOYER MIND

From Genesis 24:1, 35, we see that Abraham worked for no one. He was an employer whom God blessed in all things and had female and male servants. ***He is portrayed to have been in transport business and a commercial farmer of his time.*** The servant of Abraham (the employee for Abraham) testified that the LORD had blessed his master greatly and he had become great. He had given him property to the extent that he sent ten camels with his servant to get a get a wife for his son Isaac.

As an employer, Abraham had the following principles:

1. In Genesis14:23, he told the King of Sodom that he did not want him one day to say that he made Abraham rich. This was after rescuing Lot. He refused to get a share from the spoils. This shows that *Abraham had a rich man's mentality which does not depend on handouts*.
2. Teaching his household what is good and just. Genesis18:19.*He should have trained his household to work hard and taught them business principles.*
3. In Genesis 23, he refused to get land for burying his wife free of charge even when the owner insisted on giving it to him freely. *This confirms that he never believed in hand outs. Abraham paid for the land and got a title deed.*
4. *Abraham believed in ownership. He saw value in ownership*-in having a title deed.
5. He was not possessive, He told Lot that they were brothers and that they were not going to fight over space. *They needed to separate to create space for each other to expand as employers* (Genesis 13: 4-13).

ISAAC'S PRINCIPLES AS ONE WHO HAD AN EMPLOYER MIND

Isaac had principles as one who had an employer mind. *One of the principles he had was that of sowing seed. He knew the law of sowing and reaping and applied it in his life. He believed in investment and the multiplier effect of investment.* With these investment principles in his mind, Isaac's major secrets for his success were to do with God.

THE EIGHT SECRETS TO ISAAC'S SUCCESS AS AN EMPLOYER

There are eight identified secrets for Isaac's success which were anchored on God's promises. The following are the promises from God to Isaac that brought about his success as an employer:

1. Dwell in this land –about place from which God will bless us.
2. I will be with you –presence of God.
3. I will bless you –blessings (Psalms 37; 25).
4. I will give you land –land ownership.
5. I will perform the oath which I swore to Abraham-God's promises.
6. I will make you multiply as stars of heaven –God's involvement to multiply us or increase us (Psalms 115:15).
7. I will give your descendants all these lands.

8. In your seed all nations will be blessed.

After God spoke to him, Isaac obeyed and stayed in Gerar. Even if he wanted to go to Egypt where his father Abraham had earlier gone to during the famine of his time, Isaac was told by God not to go to Egypt. *Because he was in the right place, Isaac had to sow the seed in the midst of famine and got a hundredfold of harvest. It was this breakthrough in his investment that made him start growing his wealth to the extent that he became a wealthy man.*

JACOB'S PRINCIPLES WHEN HE WAS AN EMPLOYEE

Jacob started as an employee with his dependence on Laban as his employer. The following are some of Jacob's principles or elements in his life as an employee:

1. Hard work
2. *An employee mind*
3. Tithing- you bless me I give a tithe
4. *Depending on wages instead of owning his wealth?* **Genesis 30:30**
5. Good managerial skills
6. *Poverty*

The numbers above in bold are compared with the ones in bold below when Jacob repositioned himself as an employer

JACOB'S PRINCIPLES WHEN HE BECAME AN EMPLOYER

Despite having started as an employee, Jacob ended up being an employer and had the following principles. The following are some of Jacob's principles:

1. Hard work
2. **Having an employer mind**
3. **Transforms into being an employer**
4. Tithing- you bless me I give a tithe
5. **Ownership- Having his own wealth? Genesis 30:30**
6. When God spoke he took an action
7. Good managerial skills

THE CHARACTERISTIC OF EMPLOYERS- SEEING THE END FROM THE BEGINNING

Employers have a characteristic like that of God who sees the end from the beginning. In Isaiah 46:10-11, we are told that God sees the end from the beginning. That is how God does things. I like the way one of the languages in Zambia called Chokwe is spoken. If one is going to school he or she would not say, "I am going to school". Instead, he or she would say, "To school I am going". The person sees the end from the beginning. He or she starts with the final destination; the result-the school. He or she starts in the mind with the output before talking about the input. *Employers first see some outputs that would make them get profits.* When they have established the outputs, they then venture into looking for inputs and employees are part of the production inputs or a factor of production. *Employees on the other hand see wages as an end. They do not see profits for themselves but for their employers.* They focus on getting employed so that they can get wages. *So the question employee asks is: "How much will I be paid". The employer asks the question: "How much will I pay in order to be paid dividends?"*

We see the aspect of seeing the end from the beginning in the Lord Jesus Christ as the Son of God who sees the end from the beginning. When He started His Ministry, He had the output in mind before calling the disciples who were engaged as 'employees'. Jesus called them to as people who would be paid wages at a later stage. No wonder in Mathew19:27-29 Peter asked Jesus that they had left all to follow Him and wondered what was there for us. And Jesus assured them of wages in this life and in the life to come eternal life. *Jesus first saw the output from the ministry he had started. He was like an employer who had started an enterprise called the Church which was going to become a corporate entity on earth with a lot of wealth. He was seeing the end from the beginning.* In order to reach the end and get the output, He then ventured into mobilizing the inputs some of which were the disciples as human capital.

PLACING A HIGH VALUE ON YOURSELF AS AN EMPLOYER AS OPPOSED TO PLACING AN EMPLOYEE VALUE ON YOURSELF

Employers are investors who place a higher value on themselves than employees do. If you are to become an employer, it is important that you put high value on yourself even when others place a low value on you. For example David placed a higher value on himself after managing to kill a bear and a lion than what his brothers placed on him. After these events, *he placed a tag of a skilful fighter on himself.* If he depended on his brothers to place high value on him, he was not going to have the chance. But while his brothers devalued him, he placed a higher value on himself. David placed in his mind a high value on himself and saw the challenge at hand as an opportunity to make a difference with his value. Despite being questioned why he had gone to the battle front leaving a responsibility of keeping the animals back home, he thought he was in the right place at the right time. *No one told him that he had the ability to kill Goliath. He told himself that he was the man of the hour after identifying the need and knowing his capability.*

If you place a high value on yourself, you will not allow anyone to devalue you nor you devaluing yourself. As God's master piece, the works of his skilful hands, God the creator, the "manufacturer" placed high value on you. *Don't allow anyone to devalue you and don't devalue yourself.*

CHAPTER 4: NOT COMFORMING TO WORLD PATTERNS AND MIND RENEWAL KEY TO TRANSFORMATION

NOT COMFORMING TO THE PATTERNS OF THE WORLD AS THE STARTING POINT FOR TRANSFORMATION

In Romans 12:2 the Apostle Paul brings of four key elements that can make us have fulfilled lives here on earth:

1. Do not be conformed to the patterns of this world
2. Renew your mind
3. Be transformed
4. Prove the good, acceptable will of God.

Not conforming to the standards of this world opens the door for transformation since it becomes the basis for mind renewal to take place. Mind renewal results into transformation.

MIND RENEWAL: A BASIS FOR CHANGE LEADING TO TRANSFORMATION

Two people: Sociologist Auguste Comte has said change in type of thinking will lead to social change. Apostle Paul has pointed out that transformation will take place after not being conformed to the patterns of this world and having mind renewal. Change in thinking or mind renewal is the key on bringing about social change or transformation or development. *We need to change the way of doing things if we have to experience transformation or progress or personal development including church development and national development and business development.*

REPENTANCE IS A KEY STARTING POINT IN BRINGING ABOUT CHANGE

I have come to realize that the prerequisite to mind renewal is repentance. This takes place after refusing to conform to the patterns of this world. I use repentance here in the sense that one reaches a point of realization of the wrong direction or posture or position. At this point he or she comes back to his or her senses and makes a U-turn or changes his or her position or direction. In going in the new direction or taking up a different position from the old one, one starts renewing his or her mind after repentance. The result brings about a change in type of thinking and this change in thinking affects one's actions and hence the results.

YOU ARE A PRODUCT OF YOUR THINKING

The Bible in Proverbs23:7-8 says that man is as he thinks. It talks of what a man thinketh versus what he ends up becoming. *We are actually a product of our thoughts. In every business transaction, what we get out of it is a product of our thoughts.* Both the employer and the employee are in a business transaction of some type. One is buying and the other is selling. The employer buys the labour at a cost while the employee sells the labour at a price called wage or salary. *The aspect of being an employee or an employer is a mind issue. As you think so shall you be either an employee or an employer.*

TRANSFORMATION RESULTING FROM CHANGE

The good news is that thoughts can be changed. When you're thinking changes everything changes. Stephen Covey has written a Book entitled Change Your Thinking Change Your Life. *When you have a change in your thought life called paradigm shift, you experience transformation in that area of life in which you have made a change.* Bob Proctor talks about paradigms as being terror barriers that prevent people from doing things that they know could bring transformation in their lives. He points out that a shift in one's paradigm acts as a source of transformation in the life of such a person.

The case of Jacob in Laban's Enterprise shows us two economic conditions within the same environment. One condition was that of a person who depended on wages and life was simply of sustenance given the growth in the size of the family. The other condition was that of abundance. But this happened within the same environment. What was wrong in the first condition Jacob experienced? Was it Laban who was wrong or the economic conditions which were wrong? Or was it the fact that Jacob was not skilled enough for him to get a higher pay from Laban? What could explain Jacob's state? *What we can deduce from Jacob's failure to transition from the first condition to the second condition at first is that it was Jacob to blame. He was to blame not for having wrong skills or for being in a wrong environment but for his type of thinking at that time. His skills were right and the environment though harsh was ripe for his prosperity.* All along he had an employee mind. ***When he substituted it with an employer mind, a turnaround in his status took place within a short period.*** This was very dramatic for a man who struggled for many years before his change in type of thinking.

A CASE OF TURNAROUND IN JACOB'S ECONOMIC STATUS

Jacob experienced a turnaround in his economic position came as a result of repositioning himself from having an employee mind to having an employer mind. ***It was not until when Jacob's thinking like an employee changed to thinking like an employer (like Laban) did he see God's purpose regarding his wellbeing being fulfilled in his life.*** The verse Genesis 30:43 only became a reality when Jacob repositioned himself. The verse says that thus the man became exceedingly prosperous and had large flocks, female and male servants and camels and donkeys.

What we see in this verse regarding Jacob is that:
1. ***The man become exceedingly prosperous.***
2. His prosperity was seen in him having:
    (i)   large flocks
    (ii) female and male servants (employees)
    (iii) Camels and donkeys (transport facilities).

The question is: How did this become a reality for Jacob? ***Jacob repositioned himself in his mind as an employer. He created something in his mind which led to him making wealth. His turnaround was when he stopped thinking and acting as an employee of Laban to thinking that he also had the ability to be like uncle Laban*** –that he needed to apply the business acumen that he possessed for years. He moved further from just working hard for Laban to making profit by becoming an employer-by owning some female and male servants working and making money for him. Jacob's turnaround came from the thinking he had which led to the conversation he had with Laban in Genesis 30:25-26. It came when Jacob said to Laban:

1. Send me away-retire me
2. Retire me so that I can go to my own place and to my country.
3. Give me my resources that I have acquired while working for you.
4. For you know the services I have done for you.

So what could have been ringing in Jacob's mind before confronting Laban regarding his position? What I see from the conversation are the following points:

1. The first point about him telling Laban to send him away is to deal with freedom. This is to use one's ideas and time without control from the employer.
2. The second point about him talking about his place and his country points to the aspect of ownership. *"My place, my country-my own"*. Landlords have powers which the tenants do not have. I call it landlord power. *An employer is like the landlord and an employee is like a tenant.* Laban owned the land-the means of production and Jacob had the skills, knowledge and experience. He was also owned by Laban as a means of Laban's production (Labour).
3. *Jacob knew the value of resources in terms of skills and experience he had acquired having worked for over fourteen years for Laban.* In terms of material resources, he had little to talk about. At least he had the two wives and the children. *To Jacob this was human capital for investment which he had acquired.* He valued human capital at his disposal-his two wives and children. He also valued his knowledge, skills and experience and saw that if he was to be his own boss, God would bring a turnaround in his situation. Jacob had also acquired another form of capital called trust. He had reached a level where Laban his employer could not let him go away because of what he was able to do which gained him trust.
4. What could have rang into Jacob's mind, making him come to his senses like the prodigal son in Luke 15, were the services he had done for Laban. Again Jacob could have done some stock taking regarding the services that he had rendered to Laban. *What could have come to his mind could have been questions like this: what if the services rendered to Laban were rendered to me? Possible answer: 'What is Laban's wealth could have been mine and I would have been a wealth man.''* Fine but this is water under the bridge. Now going forward: *'What if I stopped rendering my services to Laban and rendered them to myself with God being with me, wouldn't I be a wealthy man?' Possible answer: "Yes I would be a wealthy man since the God to whom I made a vow at Bethel is a faithful God. And through my managerial abilities with which He has made me transform Laban's company to where it is.* The same God can transform me from where I am to being a wealthy Jacob."
5. What we see is that Jacob valued his true worth in Laban's company and what this worth was to him if he had his own investments. *What we also see is that Jacob compared the value of the time he spent in Laban's company getting wages to the value of the same time if it was spend on his own investment.*
6. *He could have done some stock taking of the available resources-both tangible and intangible resources.* Given these resources and

God's blessings upon him, God's favour on him and the potential in him and having perceived that Laban had his business grow because of him, ***Jacob concluded he was well able to go and apply these ideas he had on his own investment.***

7. Jacob valued an employer's wealth compared with an employee's wealth. ***An employee is a giver of services to the employer and the employer is a receiver of services from the employee.*** In making wealth the one who gains is the receiver (employer) of services compared to the giver (employee) of services. But does this not contradict with Luke 6:38? Not at all. ***Actually the striking revelation here is that both the employer and the employee are givers.*** The difference is in what they give that differentiates what they receive. ***The employer gives more investments and the more investments he or she gives, the more returns to investments he receives*** (like uncle Laban)-profit resulting in dividends. ***The employee gives out services (like Jacob). The more services he gives, the more wages he gets.*** The more he gives in terms of labour, the more skills he may end up acquiring (He/she gets more capacity built) to render better services to the employer. In the employer-employee relations, the difference is in what each of them does. One plants capital (the employer) and the other waters the capital (the employee). ***Although both of them gain, the one who plants (invests) has a greater reward because he undertook the act of creation and the other one was simply watering another's plant.***

8. What we learn from Jacob is his valuations of the position in which he was to that of Laban. ***Laban was the investor-the employer. What Jacob came up with in his mind was a change in location from being wage earner to being profit/divided earner-the returns to investment.*** The result of his valuation was that he came up with his 'business plan' and then he presented to Laban his idea to leave and go and implement his plan. We see this in the statement he made to Laban in Genesis 30:30 to say that what Laban had before he came was little but it had increased to a great extent. The Lord had blessed Laban since Jacob's coming into his company. Jacob then asked Laban when he was going to provide for his family. He then looked at the now and wondered when would also provide for his house? ***The question is: What was Jacob doing to his family for him to talk about providing for them at this point in time?***

9. In Corinthians3:6-8 Paul puts up a very important principle. He brings out three people namely:
    (i) Himself Paul (planter/farmer)
    (ii). Appolos (watering the plants).

(ii) God (specialised in making the plants grow and brings about increase.

Put another way, God provides the seed to Paul, Paul plants the seed into the ground. Appolos waters the seed to make it germinate and grow. God partners with the two and bring about increase. God is the owner of the enterprise. What insight do we get from this? The one who waters (the labourer) is not the source of the initiative. Of course he or she gets a wage for the job well done. **If we think in terms of profit, the owner of the seed gets the lion's share.** In this case God gets the glory followed by the one who got the seed and had the idea to plant it (Paul). Then the one who waters-who manages the seed gets his reward of good management (Apollos).

This same principle applies to investment. The investors or shareholders may not be the ones who do the actual work. They employ people to work for them. Those they employ to work for them as managers also employ those who have the skills to transform the resources into finished products which are then sold for cash. *Ultimately the owners of capital get the biggest reward in the value chain of production and selling.*

You need then to realize that it pays to position yourself where you have to be. You need to decide to plant the seed, as an employer, so that you benefit from the fruit rather than simply watering someone's seed, as an employee. You need to change your position so that you become a seed sower-an investor who benefits from the dividends instead of tending another's investments for wages.

JACOB REPOSITIONED HIMSELF TO BE AN EMPLOYER.

Interesting enough for Jacob, he initially found himself in an employee position despite his grandfather and his father having been employers. While in Laban's company and having worked for many years as an employee, Jacob struggled to make ends meet. He worked simply for sustenance. *It was not until when he started thinking about his hard work in connection with his gains that he made a decision to reposition himself.*

First Jacob saw himself as having been a good manager over Laban's Estate. He told Laban to let him go to his country given that Laban had known his service which he had given to him. In Genesis 30:26-30, Jacob valued the many years that he worked for Laban and the service he gave to him. He saw how much the over fourteen years had worked brought to Laban in terms of growth in his investment compared to when he joined him. Remember their employment terms started in Genesis29:15 when Laban, a business minded person, told Jacob he needed to get into an employment contract. The first contract consisted of working for a wife for seven years. *He saw himself being the major factor in the growth of Laban's investment despite being in a poverty state. He saw himself having been a good manager who brought a turnaround in Laban's business despite his poverty-stricken state.* He thought through and came to his right senses and decided to reposition himself in his mind from having an employee mind to having an employer mind. The result is what happened between Genseis30:25 and Genesis30:43. This further resulted in what we read in Genesis30:43. *You, like Jacob, need to come to your senses to bring out the employer in you. Reposition yourself to be an employer.*

Jacob's turnaround first took place in his mind as portrayed in Genesis 30:25. *He never got the right share of the fruit of his business acumen in over 14 years while working for Laban until when his thinking changed. His change in his thinking brought about a turnaround in his life from an employee to an employer. It is this change in thinking that brought a difference in his life from having only wives and children to having wealth (Genesis30:43).* What did Jacob not do in the first period for over 14 years that he did in the last period of about six years before he left Laban? For your own information, Jacob worked for Laban for a total of twenty years (Genesis31:38).*The difference or the turnaround in Jacob's affairs/ business came when he came up with mind creations/inventions and repositioned himself in his mind.* Further, *he took steps to actualize what he had devised in his mind. Tangible results were seen in his economic position and things were never the same for him again.*

WHAT JACOB DID TO TRANSFORM HIMSELF FROM HAVING AN EMPLOYEE MIND TO HAVING AN EMPLOYER MIND

The following points help us to see what Jacob might have done to transform himself from having an employee mind to having an employer mind:
1. He recalled Laban's wealth as having been little yes back when he came in and then saw himself being the beginning of Laban's growth in wealth. *He saw himself as a big factor in the growth of Laban's business and being the reason for the increase in Laban's wealth.*
2. He saw God's involvement in making Laban's wealth grow because of him (Jacob). He realized that he had made a vow to God in Genesis28:20-22 and that *God was faithful and worth being counted on for a turnaround.* He also saw himself carrying the blessing of Abraham and that of his father Isaac. *He could*

have wondered why he was living like a pauper when actually he was a prince.
3. His coming into Laban's company brought God's involvement. *The God factor blessed Jacob but the benefits of the blessing went to Laban who owned Jacob the labourer.*
4. He saw himself as being a good manager. *Despite him being a good manager and a main factor in the increase of Laban's wealth, Jacob should have seen the principle behind ownership of the investment-Laban the owner was the major beneficiary.*
5. He saw that *with time wealth grows as a result of good management* and he was that good manager behind the growth in the wealth of Laban.
6. He saw that despite the increase in the wealth of Laban associated to a greater extent to result of his labour (Jacob's labour), the one who was smiling was Laban. *Laban was now making money while seated and while Jacob was watching.*
7. *He valued his personal worth in Laban's business* and what he had put in the business in form of human capital.
8. *He pictured what this worth in him would mean to him if he was to use it in his own enterprise and benefit from the shareholder's worth-the dividends.* He was now *looking at himself as human capital to be paid dividend and not a human resource that gets paid a wage or salary.* He also *saw himself as having accumulated social capital-trust.*
9. *He imagined how it would be if he was the owner of the business* and what amount of wealth he would have got in the over fourteen years that he worked for Laban.
10. *He refused to accept the state in which he was as an employee getting peanuts to remain a permanent state. He needed to reposition himself as an employer* knowing that this is how you become wealthy.
11. *He started by repositioning himself in his mind to having an employer mind.* An employee's mind perspective is different from that of an employer. *The perspective (the thinking) of the employee determines what he or she gets at the end of the day. The employer's thinking also determines what he gets ultimately.*
12. *He reasoned that now the hour had come for him to go into ownership in order to provide for his family.* The question as asked above is: If he was now to provide for his family what then was he doing all the years he worked for Laban? (Genesis 30:30).
13. *He then made a bold decision to launch his retirement plan from Laban's company. His decision intimately determined his wealth that he ended up acquiring.* Dr Murdock has said *your decisions*

determine your wealth. He says nothing but your decision determines joy. Decisions determine income, decision determine strength. If you realise it is your decisions that decides your wealth nothing will stop you from becoming an employer, a wealth person as long as you live. Jacob's decision changed his situation forever.

14. *He resolved to start his own enterprise.* At most he resolved to leave Laban. But Laban was not ready to let him go because he was gaining from him as an employee. *Somehow a way out was to be found for him to start creating wealth for himself now with an employer mind.*
15. He planned to present his manifesto to Laban. It brought him into a better negotiation position with Laban Genesis 30:30. *He finally acted by communicating his decision to Laban.*
16. *His decision and action increased his bargaining power with Laban and made him reap wealth from Laban's company since the law of operation had changed.* That is *the law of being an employee who gets a wage or a salary to the law of an employer who shares in dividends.* Remember that *both the employee and the employer are employing something but the difference is in what they each sow and what each reaps. This makes them end up having different results.*
17. He managed to bargain for a fair deal with Laban that would later result in the wealth of Laban being transferred to him. *The bargain was no longer at an employee basis but at an employer basis. Going forward, they were to share in the proceeds of the animals and not in wages.* The collective agreement should have been turned into a shareholder partnership deed or company rules.
18. *His decision and actions moved him to the next level of wealth.* As a result, *he was transformed from being a cost of production in the books of account for Laban to being on the asset side.* Remember that as an employee you are a cost of production in the books of account of your employer. A wage or a salary is entered in the Profit and Loss account as a cost or a liability to the employer. That is why *the aim of an employer is to minimize cost and maximize shareholder returns.* A shareholder gets paid when profits are declared in the profit and loss account and dividends are declared after dealing with the liabilities which include wages or salaries. The shareholder benefit more than employees. That is why *it pays to be an employer rather than being an employee who is a cost of production to the employer.*
19. *His desire to change his situation made the change to take place. Hating your current state of affairs is the beginning of*

transformation in your life. *When you say enough is enough that is the beginning of change in your mind and hence mind renewal which leads to transformation.*
20. He had confidence in God making him successful. *He relied on God's faithfulness and commitment to His promises.*
21. *His decision and action made his final story be like that of his grandfather Abraham and like his that of his father Isaac.* These patriarchs were employed by nobody but they were themselves employers. *We are told about Abraham in Genesis 24:34-35 that he was a rich man at the same time being a man of faith –a friend of God. God blessed him in everything (Genesis24:1).* He had employees, donkeys and camels which in today's economy we can say he was a transporter and a commercial famer. His father Isaac invested (sowed a seed) and had a hundred fold harvest because God had blessed him (Genesis 26:12-14).*We see Isaac's investment growing until he became a very wealth person so that non-believers envied him and went to him to make covenants with him because he had become powerful.* But *if Jacob had not decided to reposition himself, his story would have remained on the opposite side of his grandfather's and his father's stories of faith plus wealth.*
22. *He ultimately became an employer-wealthy man. He saw his wealth grow until his story changed.* He now had flocks, camels and men and female servants. *Gensesis30:43 concludes the matter with the word: Thus, or in this way or then, or therefore or as a result or and. This means that this was a result of some step(s) or action(s) being taken.*

WHAT LED TO JACOB'S TURNAROUND IN WEALTH AND BROUGHT A DIFFIRENCE IN HIS STATUS?

He repositioned himself from having the employee mind to having an employer mind. Young people, especially, need to develop an employer mind. This will set them apart from their peers. In a book entitled the richest man in Babylon, the man who later became a horse trader was first challenged by the wife and his master to *have the mind of a free man instead of the mind of a slave. When you're thinking changes, everything changes.*

Genesis 30:43 became a reality in Jacob's life because of his change of attitude from being an employee to having a mind of an employer. *He changed from being a receiver of wages to being a receiver of dividends.*

WHAT LED TO THE RESULTS REALIZED BY JACOB IN GENESIS30:43

"You can't travel within and stand still without." James Allen

"The person you see yourself in your mind today is the person you will see tomorrow." Sam Adeyemi- Paraphrased

Applying these quotes to the employer in you, we can learn a lot from the mind renewal that took place inside Jacob's mind. *As he travelled within himself, this resulted in the transformation of himself from being an employee to being an employer.* Before approaching uncle Laban, Jacob had travelled far in his mind in his endeavour to become an employer. He should have visualized himself owning what Laban owned as an employer. *The man had traversed distances in his mind, imagined what he could be if he repositioned himself by being an employer. He saw a lot in his mind as mental pictures and had a vision of his better future before approaching uncle Laban.* Finally after travelling within, he was able to automatically travel without. *His outlook and his situation changed without after changing within.* This is according to what the Bible says that as a man thinks so is he. *Jacob became the result of his thoughts. You results are a reflection of what you are inside.*

BETWEEN GENESIS 30:25 AND GENESIS30:43

For me, what came as a powerful revelation to me, like bright light shining in my heart, was when one day I compared what happened between Genesis 30:25 and Genesis30:43. I realized that the transformation that took place in the life of Jacob as regards wealth was as a result of his change in type of thinking. This took place before Genesis30:25. AS already referred to, Sociologist Auguste Comte pointed out that change in type of thinking can lead to social change. For Jacob, this change took place tremendously. *It is like over fourteen years that Jacob didn't act in this manner, he was delaying God from making the blessings that he carried in him from being made tangible.* It is clear that *God was blessing him and the blessings were made tangible but landed on the employer since he was, in his mind and action, in the employee position. This was the tragedy for Jacob and the situation would have continued like this for the whole of his life if he did not reposition himself in his mind.*

In between Genesis30:25 and Genesis30:43, we see the result of Jacob making up his mind to reposition himself from having an employee mind to having the employer mind. What I have come to call drama that took place between Genesis 30:25 and Genesis30:43 is the reason for the conclusion in Genesis30:43. When you critically analyse the way verse 43 comes out, it is telling us that if Jacob had not repositioned himself in his mind, his state was going to remain the same or even worse off without realizing verse43. But *thanks be to God who came to him in a dream and told him that he had seen what Laban had done to him and gave him a revelation for becoming rich.* May God give you and me such a revelation in a dream or any other channel that He may use. *I believe that the transformation in Jacob's mind was God's working in his life.* Since he co-operated with God and made Him a partner in his plans (Proverbs16:1,3,9) as well as during his implementation, God established the work of his hands and gave him success as a result of making God his "business partner" (Psalms90:15-16). May He do the same in your life and mine.

The situation between Genesis30:25 and Genesis30:43 was so dramatic that it left Laban and his family shocked to see how quickly the man Jacob who was poor was becoming rich This can be seen in the reaction from Laban and his family as pointed out in Genesis31:1-5. Laban and his family saw their wealth going to Jacob as they watched with their eyes. *This was possible because Jacob took a unique decision that put him in a better position to bargain in order to share in the proceeds from the animals.* Jacob even went to the extent of deciding the colours he wanted after God revealed the colours to him in a dream. I like the way Genesis 30:43 concludes about the transformation that took place in Jacob's life from poverty to riches and to wealth. It says **THUS**. Put another way, one can say *as a result of the repositioning* in his mind and the actions he took, he moved from poverty as portrayed in Genesis30:25-29 to being a wealthy man. I like the way the story ends in a dramatic manner- God transferring wealth from Laban to Jacob to reward him for his decision, action and good management. This was not going to happen without Jacob repositioning himself in his mind.

You know what? God is faithful. He was faithful to Jacob. He is still a faithful to you and me if we do our part. He is worth trusting and entrusting our affairs to Him. *When we make vows to him like Jacob did in Genesis28:20-22 and live by our vows, God is so faithful that He can bring drama in our lives and change our poverty state to riches if we do not conform to the patterns of the world and have mind renewal.* See how faithful God was to God: He reminded Jacob in Genesis31:13 that He was the God of Bethel where Jacob anointed a pillar and made a vow to Him. It looks like God was congratulating Jacob for having kept and fulfilled the vow. This can be seen in God's statement where He said He had seen Jacob's mistreatment by Laban and that God had come to intervene. *May God also intervene in your situation and my situation.*

Before Genesis30:25 Laban's thinking was more superior to that of Jacob in that *Laban displayed an employer mind while Jacob displayed an employee mind for many years. This made Laban progress in his capital formation while Jacob remained in the same state apart from having an increase in his family size.* His economic situation of depending on wages deteriorated as his responsibilities grew while depending on one source of revenue namely wages. But between Genesis 30:25 and Genesis30:43 things turned around and Jacob's thinking became superior to that of Laban. *It is this superior thinking that made Jacob operate at a higher level such that he ended up amassing the wealth which otherwise would have been for Laban had he not repositioned himself.* We see that Jacob repositioned his mind and brought about transformation in his life. Of course all this was possible with God Almighty's involvement.

From the time Jacob got into the enterprise of Jacob up until in Genesis30:25, Jacob never made progress in terms of his wealth status. What he had to talk of really were the two wives and the children that he acquired and nothing else. This was despite his input into Jacob's business. *He worked hard all the years he was with Laban for over fourteen years and like Ecclesiastes 10:15 puts it he turned out to be a fool. Why a fool? This is so because he did not fully benefit from his labour.* The situation would have continued to be the same had he not acted the way he did starting from Gensesis30:25 until he got the results in Genesis30:43. His actions during this short period of the last six years with Laban out of the twenty years with him made a huge difference in his life.

As already pointed out, what brought the difference in Jacob's life was *the difference in thinking of ownership as an employer and that of the thinking as an employee who aims at getting wages.* Before Genesis30:25, Jacob spent many years working for Laban and he had reaped little until in Genesis30:25 when *a dramatic change took place in the mind of Jacob. Take note that it is the issue of the mind. The same man Jacob who spent over 14 years with no progress in his working career ended up making a difference between Genesis30:25 and Genesis30:43.* The environment remained the same but the results were different. *It is his thinking which changed within the same environment and ended up giving him different results in the same area he worked for years.* Just imagine! *If his thinking did not change, his situation wouldn't have changed. He started seeing differently in his mind.* He saw the beauty of having an employer mind, as one doing his own things. He saw that God had the ability to make him rich if only he had the required thinking that brings riches and take the appropriate action

In Genesis 13:14-15, God told Abraham to see, arise, walk through the land and make it his. In Joshua6:2, God told Joshua to see that He had given him Jericho. *What we see from these scriptures is that what God ends up giving us what we see and the steps we take to acquire what we see. When we have mind renewal and make decisions to make God partner with us in bringing about transformation, we end up proving the good, acceptable and perfect will of God. The principle here is that God gives us to the extent that we see. If we see ourselves as grasshoppers, we become like them in our minds and we do not go anywhere. If we see ourselves as giants, we become giants in our minds and end up being victorious in our lives.*

If Jacob was to remain content with his job in Laban's company, he was not going to see the difference. *The change; the transformation; the turnaround that came to take place in his life only happened when he asked himself a question, "When am I my going to work for my own family?"*. I believe he had first asked himself this question and gave an answer to it before he asked Laban the same answer. I believe so because this can be seen from the strategy he took to make Laban agree to his terms as pointed out in Genesis30:30-34. It takes one who had spent time thinking about the situation and imagining what it takes to have something done for the sake of one's family. So *what we see between Genesis30:25 and Genesis30:43 are transformation actions that led to a turnaround.* Jacob started by not conforming to the standard of him being an employee and Laban remaining in an Employer position. He needed to reposition himself by refusing to be conformed to the pattern he had entertained for years. He then had mind renewal which resulted in transformation. The result was that he ultimately proved the good, acceptable perfect will of God (Romans12:2).

The following are the insights we can get from Jacob's repositioning:

1. We see Jacob realizing that it does not pay much to be an employee. *Being an employee makes you end up being undervalued and hence underpaid.* Secondly, we see that before Genesis30:25, Jacob underwent some pain in his heart of working for someone and seeing him prosper while he remained stagnant. *Stagnation or having progressing only a little is a painful thing. We are designed for progress in life. So if we are not progressing in what we are doing, it must make us get seriously concerned.* From what Jacob said to him Laban, we see that *it is very painful when you realize how much you know you have worked for somebody and you see his wealth grow under your care.* Meanwhile, you get peanuts and see your situation deteriorating or simply you experiencing bare sustenance from what you get from your labour. *To say the least this is more painful when you realize that you were meant for progress.* It has been said that if you see things normal, you may not change your situation. ***People who change their current situation are those who hate the state in which they are and make a bold decision to change it.***

For many years Jacob saw the bad state in which he was and never took any action and things remained the same. ***The difference was made when he reached a state when he hated his status quo. Genesis30:25 going forward made a difference that transformed his life forever. You and I can make a difference when like Jacob we say enough is enough.***

2. We see Jacob taking a bold and calculated step to reposition himself from being an employee to ***having an employer mind that looks at owning the means of production.*** Fourth, we see Jacob's better thinking making him strategic in his actions and ending up convincing Laban who seemed to be a 'hard' man.

3. We see Jacob's ability to bargain working to his advantage at this time. Remember this is the same man who was able to bargain for a birth right with his brother some years back and managed to get it using soup. ***What was in him which he seemed not to utilize as much as he could was his ability to bargain.*** Now the hour had come for him to bring transformation in his life because he had renewed his mind. ***Transformation can only come in your life when your mind is renewed.*** Regarding this matter, Jacob's mind had been renewed leading to him taking steps he never took for years. ***Mind renewal made a huge difference in his life going forward.***

4. ***We see Jacob setting up an investment portfolio for himself*** within Laban's enterprise and starting accumulating wealth that he failed to accumulate for over fourteen years. He made a growth in his net worth in terms of wealth in the last part of his twenty years working for Laban. This was in the last period of about six years that he brought about transformation.

5. ***We see God getting involved by an angel appearing to Jacob in a dream.*** Now where was God all along? Why did God not appear to him before he bargained for getting a share from the proceeds from Laban's animals. Of course, God was with him through and through. ***But at this particular moment we see God acting in a special manner by giving him a genetic formula in a dream.*** At the same time he reminds Jacob about the vow he made to Him (God) at Bethel (Genesis28:20-22). ***This shows that all along God wanted to bless Jacob beyond measure but Jacob did not create a platform for God***

to act. Now that Jacob had created a platform, God appeared to him in a dream in Genesis31:10-13.* What an amazing thing! So then *even me I can sense that God should have been waiting for me to create a platform for Him to appear to me and give me a dream for my breakthrough to prosperity.* But alas, I am the one who has been letting God down all along. Shame to me! I don't know for you. *Now to make me a proud man, I have to create a platform for God to make the blessings upon me tangible.*

6. *We see Jacob taking a step of faith to act and put into practice what he saw in a dream revealed to him by God.* Apart from seeing in the dream, Jacob heard the angel of God speaking to him. The Bible says the just shall live by faith, but faith without works is dead. We are also told that we should not simply be hearers but doers of what we hear lest we be like one who looks into the mirror and thereafter forgets how he or she looks like (2 Corinthians5:7;James1:22-25; 2:20). *We are blessed if we act on what we hear God telling us. This was the secret for Jacob's breakthrough and turnaround. It was also the secret for his father Isaac and his grandfather Abraham. These men listened to God attentively and thereafter acted accordingly and immediately*. This was the secret for their success. You and I can emulate them.

7. Jacob's thinking changed before he saw the wealth in Genesis 30:43. *He saw the wealth from the invisible before he saw the wealth visibly. He simply started with an idea that led him into taking steps that made the idea be transformed into tangible results.*

8. What we see in Jacob is the putting into practice the principle of multiplication as portrayed in Gensis1:28. He was fruitful but the fruit he produced contributed to the multiplication of Laban's wealth. *Now between Genesis30:25 and Genesis30: 43, Jacob was not only fruitful but he multiplied his fruitfulness for his sake and the sake of his family.* We see his wealth multiplying. Thanks be to God the supplier of seed who supplies us with seed and multiplies it to increase our store of seed (2 Corinthians9:10-11). *In business terms God multiplies our capital as we engage in business transactions for ourselves because He is interested in our prosperity just like he was interested in Jacob's prosperity.*

9. *We see the God-hand in Jacob's business affairs*. As Jacob narrates to his wives in Genesis31:7-9, he saw the hand of God as God intervened in his favour between Genesis30:25 and Genesis30:43.Despite Laban changing goal posts every now and then,

Jacob said that *it was the hand of God that made a difference in his success. God's hand in your life will make a difference in your success and mine too.*

10. We see Jacob telling his wives that God had taken away the wealth of their father and given it to him (Genesis31:9). Again one wonders why God did not transfer the wealth of Laban to him before Genesis 30:25. Jacob brings out the secret for God transferring the wealth of the wicked to us in Genesis30:10. *God transfers wealth to us by us having something that produces fruitfulness. When we do this God partners with us and gets interested in our ideas and as such provides seed and continues to multiply the seed we sow.* For Jacob, in the breeding season, he once had a dream in which he looked up and saw that the male goats mating with the flock were streaked, speckled or spotted. He saw the three colors during the breeding season (Genesis30:10). *During the breeding season! This is the key time. It was during the season of productivity that he saw the formula from God. God is interested in productivity. He wants you to be productive.* For this reason *when you start productivity ventures, you need to be conscious of the fact that your Father in heaven gets involved (Proverbs16:9).* You only let Him down when you become a poor manager and waste the resources He gives you to invest and manage.

11. Jacob is said to have been a very good manager before Genesis30:25. He himself tells Laban so and Laban himself confesses the same. Laban gives what we may call a testimony of how the coming in of Jacob made a noticeable difference in his enterprise (Genesis30:27-30). *His wealth grew and he saw a lot of progress because of Jacob's good managerial skills.* But to whose benefit? It was more to the benefit of Laban and not Jacob who was the reason for the turnaround in Laban's business. *Your good management will benefit you more when you direct it towards your own investment.* This is what we see in Jacob between Genesis30:25 and Genesis30:43.

12. From what Laban told Jacob, it was not only that Jacob was a good manager, but that Laban saw the God factor as we have already stated above. *Laban does not say that God has blessed him simply because of Jacob's business acumen alone but that God blessed him for the sake of Jacob.* What does this mean? *Jacob was a man carrying a blessing on him. The fact that you carry a blessing and that you have the God factor in your life makes your employer prosper when you are in his organization.* From this confession by Laban, Jacob could

have got a revelation that *if the God factor on him had made this man prosper, then God would prosper him if he had his own enterprise.*

13. Laban saw his wealth going to Jacob without any room of calling him a thief. Jacob had got his wealth legally. The legality was based on the three colors that Jacob agreed with Laban as a share from the work he did. You know what? *God is looking for a legal arrangement within which He can perform wonders for you. Take note that this transfer of wealth happened within the same environment in which both of them transacted for many years. This time the rules of the game had changed and as such Jacob ended up being a winner out of this game.*

14. *We see the power of dreams and visions at work between Genesis30:25 and Genesis30:43.* Normally *if you pursue what you see in a dream or vision, you end up making it become a reality if you don't give up along the way.* Despite the fact that you may meet killers of vision along the way, the chances are that God being with you, the dream or vision you have will come to pass. *For Jacob the three colors were first seen in a dream (Gensesis31:10-13). When he woke up he acted on the dream and he saw the reality come true.* His wealth grew exceedingly and his life was transformed materially.

15. We are finally told that the man Jacob increased. His increase could be seen tangibly. *The man ended up owning what he never owned for many years.* It is recorded that *Jacob grew exceedingly prosperous and came to own large flocks, maidservants and menservants, camels and donkeys.* The result was that the countenance of Laban changed because *he saw the man he kept in poverty for many years prospering. Laban's sons also started protesting because they saw Jacob progressing from having little to having plenty. They saw the law of sowing and reaping at work in the life of Jacob.* Remember that as your wealth grows you are likely to meet some criticisms. But if God is for you who can against you?

16. Genesis30:43 uses terms like 'In this way'; 'Thus'; 'As a result' to indicate that there is something that happened before that brought about the outcome. *The question you ask yourself is: what exactly happened that led to this positive outcome? There are steps that Jacob took without which there would not have been this result. The repositioning that took place in his mind; the step he took in confronting his employer that he wanted to leave; the bargaining with Laban; the dream about the three colors being put in practice;*

the setting up his own investment, among others, made a huge difference in his life. For Jacob, as we have pointed out above, we see that the outcome of his steps is that the man grew exceedingly prosperous and came to own large flocks, maidservants and menservants, camels and donkeys. The law of sowing and reaping was at work. A man reaps what he sows. *Life then is about sowing and reaping but the type and quality of seed we sow makes a difference.* Given the steps that he took Jacob got the results that he had.

17. *We see that before Genesis30:25, nothing was growing on Jacob's side except the size of his family and the cost of living becoming higher each day. Jacob simply depended on wages which Laban continued changing not for better but for worse.* On the other side for Laban, *his investments were growing exponentially as a result of a combination of Jacob's managerial skills and God's covenant blessing on him as a descendant of Abraham. What should have been his blessing landed on Laban who owned the means of production.* This should have been painful to a man who years back built an altar before God at Bethel where he put the burden of his prosperity on God (Genesis28:20-22). *As long as we do not do our part, we make God not do His part.* We see this in Jacob that *despite the vows he made to God and making God get committed that day from Bethel onwards, God could not do much because Jacob's actions limited God's actions.* Remember that Jesus was also limited in performing many miracles for lack of faith in some places. In the same way, *we limit God's performing wonders in our lives when we do not do our part. Do your part and then God will come in to do His part. John 13:17 is always touching me with Jesus' words that we will be blessed if we do the things we know. This is what Jacob did after failing God for many years of inactivity in terms of putting up his own investment.* We see between Genesis30:25 and Genesis30:43 that *God intervened immediately Jacob set up his own enterprise. He then appeared to him in a dream during the breeding season (Genesis31:10-13). The story for Jacob changed dramatically as a result of him doing something that made God do His part as regards Jacob's business undertakings.*

18. *Between Genesis30:25 and Genesis30:43, Jacob saw the principle of wealth accumulation. He should have realized that wealth accumulates from a particular base. Without laying a foundation, you do not see a house being built.* In the same way, *wealth can only be accumulated from a particular laid foundation.* It then starts growing from this foundation from little to plenty. *Jacob assessed*

Laban's wealth growth and leaned that it grew from little to plenty with years. He realized that *if he was to start from somewhere, he would change his situation.* His putting up an investment base would make him join the group of people whose wealth grew from little to plenty. He had observed this phenomena working regarding Laban's wealth. He should have realized out of this experience that if he took a similar step like what others had done, he would be like them in wealth acquisition and accumulation. *He then took a step in this direction and the result is what we read in Gensesis30:43. This is the secret of an employer mind as opposed to the employee mind.*

FULFILLMENT OF GENESIS30:43: WHAT MADE THIS VERSE BECOME A REALITY?

It is repositioning that made Genesis30:43 become a reality. Jacob repositioned himself in his mind and this repositioning had with it strategies formulated and strategic actions taken to make the strategies a reality. The results for Jacob are recorded in Genesis30:43 and the proceeding actions taken by Jacob that led to the results are recorded between Genesis30:25-42. *Starting of Genesis30:43 with the word Thus to conclude the story speaks volumes about what led to the transformation in Jacob's status from simply being a wage earner to someone owning flocks, camels, donkeys and employees (male servants and female servants).* Genesis30:25-43 teaches us that *we also can change our status through mind renewal that brings repositioning resulting in transformation.* It tells you and me the importance of the mind and mind repositioning if we want to see a change in our lives. *Just imagine Jacob changing his status in a period of about less than six years compared to fourteen years when he was just a wage earner and yet working hard!*

GENESIS30:43 IS EVIDENCE THAT JACOB TRANSFORMED HIMSELF FROM BEING A POOR WISE MAN TO BEING A RICH WISE MAN

Many of us are poor wise men and women. According to Ecclasiastes9:13-16, we are told the story of a poor wise man. This poor wise man using his wisdom saved a small city that was conquered by a strong king. *After saving the city, the poor wise man was forgotten. In this regard, we are told that although wisdom is better than might, the wisdom of commoners is despised and they are not taken note of.*

In January 2017, I attended a programme where Pastor Mensah Otabil was one of the speakers. Actually I was made to go there specifically to listen to him since he started influencing me many years ago. He has been one of the men of God who have inspired me. Having been caught up in traffic on my way to the venue and looking for where to pack the car, I ended up listening to him speak only in the last ten minutes when I finally entered the church.

My listening to him in the ten minutes was as if I had heard him speak from the beginning. I found him talking about a poor wise man as portrayed in the scripture quoted above. Among the illustrations he gave, he mentioned *Jacob as being an example of a poor wise man. He said Laban used Jacob to make him become wealthy to the extent that he had audacity to tell Jacob it was him behind his riches* (Genesis30:27). *He said that many of us despite being wise are simply used by others, including our employers, and dumped with our poverty.*

Jacob realized that he was a poor wise man who was just being used by Laban and *he reached a stage where he refused to be a poor wise man. He then took steps to transform himself into a corporate entrepreneur and leveraged on Laban's enterprise to make Genesis30:43 become a reality.* As you read Genesis30:43, *it is evidence of a man who had transformed himself from being a poor wise man to being a rich wise man. You and I are capable of transforming ourselves from being commoners to being people of influence in society as people not only with wisdom but also with wealth.* With God and by faith all things are possible to them who believe.

CHAPTER 5: REPOSITIONING YOURSELF FROM HAVING AN EMPLOYEE MIND TO HAVING AN EMPLOYER MIND.

Like Jacob who repositioned himself from having an employee mind to having an employer mind that brought a turnaround in his wealth, you too need to do the same. *It is repositioning yourself which is the first key to bringing about a turnaround in your life.* I have so far seen it in my own life where I have found myself doing things I never dreamed I would ever do. *I am looking forward to seeing greater things taking place in my life.* Why do I say so? It is because *in my mind I have already traversed thousands of kilometres in becoming an employer.* What is remaining is *to fully actualize my becoming an employer by making things move from my mind to make them tangible. This is my heart's desire before I part from the stage called earth where God has given me an opportunity to be an actor.*

To substantiate how far I have traversed in my mind, I would like to refer to some of the statements from some of the men of God who have influenced my thinking. These have contributed greatly to the repositioning that has taken place in my mind to have an employer mind.

One day I listened to pastor Ashimolowo on **KICC** Television who said that failure to raise capacity is an indication of our under achievement. He said *you should choose to re-engineer your life.* He further said *we should not settle for little performance and little results and move to greater achievements and greater favour*. He further said we need to increase our capacity.

I also listened to Pastor David Abioyemie on the same KICC television who said *if you know how to think you will be employed if you know why you should think you will be an employer.* When I heard this I evaluated my situation and understood why I was employed. I realized that I only knew how to think hence I became an employee. *Had I known why I should think, I should have been an employer employing those who know how to think.* What this means is that both the employer and the employer think but the difference is that the *employee knows how to* while the *employer knows why to*.

WHAT IS REPOSITIONING ABOUT?

Before we talk about repositioning, we can first talk about positioning. *The position in which you are means quite a lot to what you get or end up becoming.* Look at football, when you are on the pitch playing, all players have a position they play and they all have chances of scoring but the chances of scoring are higher as one gets closer to the goal post. The position each one of them plays has an effect on the way they play on the pitch. The position is the place you take either physically or mentally. *The concept of position applies with the mind. The mind gets positioned regarding some beliefs. The way you position your mind in terms of the thoughts you entertain has an effect on the result you produce in terms of your actions.*

Now what is to reposition?

According to http://www.thefreedictionary.com/repositioning, to reposition is to place or put in a new position; position again.

Repositioning then implies:

- To put in a new position
- To change position.
- To change place or direction

The three aspects on repositioning will be applied as we go through the book. If repositioning is to put in a new position or to change position or to change place or direction, *it means that for you to make a difference in your life, you need to change position; to be put in a new position and to change place or direction.* I have come to realize that *for any meaningful change for better to take place in your life, you need to reach a point of what I call repentance.* Repentance means that you will change direction and go in a direction that will bring about transformation. This has to be complemented by what the Apostle Paul calls mind renewal in Romans 12:2. He points out that *for you to test the acceptable, good and perfect will of God here on earth, you need to start not conforming yourself to the standards (patterns) of this world followed by mind renewal.*

Mind renewal will then result in transformation. Transformation will make you test good things which are in store for you. Without renewing your mind, you cannot experience transformation and hence you will fail to prove the good, acceptable and perfect will of God. *So where do you start from? First* make an analysis of the position where you are. Then accept that you are in a wrong position. We call this in Christian circles as accepting that you have 'sinned' and confessing your 'sins'. Confessing your sins is not enough. Next you will need to repent. *You need to change direction. Without this no change will take place no matter how you crave for it. This is change of mind and change of direction.* You then have to refuse to conform to world patterns. When you change direction, you devise strategies for taking you where you want to go. *You then come up with a change management strategy which you will need to implement in your life or business situation.* This then will result in you repositioning yourself.

This applies to individual, family, community, organizational and national situations. This also applies to the subject of this book for you as an individual with the respect to what you will test in this life regarding either you being an employee or an employer. *This book: The Employer in You: Repositioning Yourself from Having an Employee mind to having an Employer Mind is about change of position starting with your mind.* It is about mind renewal that will bring about transformation from you being an employee to being an employer. Read more and reposition yourself.

ATTITUDE HAS TO DO WITH THE ALTITUDE YOU GO TO

Pastor Bill Winston says that attitude has to do with the altitude you go to. Drawing a lesson from this and connecting it to the attitudes of the employer and that of the employee, we can see that *the employer and the employee are at different altitudes in their minds. It is the altitudes they go to which makes a difference between the two.* The employer is at an altitude of ownership of the means of production while the employee is on the attitude of owning labour which he/she sells at a price called a salary or wage to the employer. The employee's behaviour is influenced by the attitude of dependence on the employer for sustenance of his/her life. The employer's behaviour is instead influenced by the attitude of independence in applying his/her business ideas to grow wealth.

MANY OF US ARE IN THE STATE IN WHICH WE ARE BECAUSE OF FEAR

"Whatever you can do or dream you can do, begin it. Boldness has genius, power and magic in it. Begin it now." W. H. Murray

It is boldness that makes a lion a king of the jungle. The Bible in Numbers 23:24 says, "Look, a people rises like a lioness and lifts itself up like a lion; it shall not lie down until it devours the prey and drinks the blood of the slain."

Although this verse is in reference to a different issue, we can pick out the character of a lion to apply it to our topic. A lion is courageous; it is bold and overcomes fear through its attitude. If you check yourself, you will realize that you might have missed an opportunity because you were afraid of taking a risk. But bear in mind that if you have to succeed, you have to be a risk taker. Of course you need to take calculated risks. I have come to learn that the higher the risk you take, the higher the returns if all goes well.

YOU NEED TO OVERCOME FEAR

At the time of writing this Book, I attended a seminar on Kingdom Entrepreneurship at Winners' Chapel in Lusaka. My daughter Ebenezer who was attending the seminar made me attend. The main speaker, a man of God from Nigeria, was teaching on Kingdom Entrepreneurship. At the end of his ministering, the Pastor of the Church quoted 2Timothy1:7 and encouraged the audience to stir up their gifts. *He said that many destinies are limited by fear. He told the audience to go beyond as global beings by being strong and courageous and possess the land.* This is what God told Joshua in Joshua chapter one not to fear but be courageous in order to possess the Promised Land.

THE GRASSHOPPER MENTALITY VERSUS GIANT MENTALITY (THE WELL ABLE MENTALITY)

Fear, dismay and discouragement take place in our minds. How we react to fear makes a difference. The Psalmist in Psalms56:3 said that when he was afraid he would trust in the Lord. *What type of mentality do you have? Is it the grasshopper mentality or giant mentality (the well able mentality)? The grasshopper mentality acknowledges all the good things they have seen but write a nevertheless report in their minds and declare that they are unable. The well able people with a giant mentality acknowledge the challenges ahead of them but instead write a report in their minds that read: Despite the challenges that face us we are well able.* This illustration is drawn from the Israelites in the wilderness who ended up being divided into two categories with respect to the types of mind they had (Numbers13:25-33). *The category of minds they had determined the output they got from their lives.* While some died in the wilderness without possessing the land God had prepared for them, the others like Caleb possessed the land by faith. *Faith is the opposite of fear. The people with a well able mentality did not just look at their limitations but leveraged on God's capabilities.*

Today we need Kingdom entrepreneurs to venture into the business arenas with boldness where they will need to overcome "giants" since they themselves are giants because they carry Jesus in themselves. These entrepreneurs have employer minds as opposed to having employee minds. You need to realize that *your mind swings between the two minds: employee mind and employer mind. The attitude of your mind determines whether you can be an employee or an employer. So the extent to which you go to in your mind and the actions you take as a result of the extent you have gone in your mind will determine what you end up becoming.* The limited results we see in our lives can be attributed to mind limitations. If we remove the mind limitations, we can see tremendous changes that can take place in our lives. We can see ourselves possessing what we may not possess in the current condition of our minds. *It is the courageous who take action who end up enjoying what is beyond what they are able to see now.*

KNOWING HOW TO THINK VERSES KNOWING WHY YOU SHOULD THINK

As I have indicated above one day I listened, on television, to the pastor of Salvation Ministries Pastor David Abioyemie speaking about the difference between an employee and an employer. This was to deal with the difference in how an employee and an employer think making a difference in the results they each finally get. As already pointed out, he pointed out that if you know how to think you will be employed but if you know why you should think you will be an employer. *This statement blew my mind as one who had worked as an employee instead of working as an employer. It revolutionized my thinking from that day onwards. The statement was like adding salt to an injury that I already had since I seemed to be dissatisfied by being an employee. This dissatisfaction in me came when I considered the idle potential in me that I had not exploited since I spent my time on the employee side without bringing out the employer in me.* From this day onwards, I realized why I was an employee and how that every time I went for further studies up to Master's Degree level it was for promotion. I understood that I only knew how to think. *Had I known why I should think I would have been an employer and my situation would have been different.*

Having seen myself as one who **knew how to think, instead of knowing why I should think**, *I understood that it did not matter how much I knew since this knowledge was being sold for a salary.* My thinking has never been the same thenceforth. With the Doctorate in Business Administration that I am currently pursuing, my motive is no longer promotion. *I want to know why I should think and become an employer before I leave this stage called earth.*

The seriousness of knowing how to think instead of knowing why we should think can be seen from a joke one workmate of mine made. He said that *despite all our education, especially those of us working for government as public servants, we become speech writers. This is the agony of the employee regardless of what he or she knows.* I realized that if *I knew why I should think*, I would not be an employee working under such circumstances.

WHAT IS THE ULTIMATE FOR GOING TO COLLEGE OR UNIVERSITY

One day a discussion regarding education came up with a colleague who asked me what the ultimate for studying was. I answered by telling him that the answer to this question depends on the side on which you are in your mind. *The ultimate is whether you are studying for being an employee whose one of the reasons for further studies is being employed and getting promotion or you are studying for the purpose of acquiring more enlightenment to help you create wealth.* The interesting thing about the majority who go to college is that they are taught to become employees and they become so or end up stranded without finding jobs.

STUDYING FOR WEALTH CREATION

If you have an employer mind then your ultimate for studying is to acquire knowledge that will help you create value which will earn you customers who will consume your product or service at a price. The one with the employer mind has the motivation for studying in order to sharpen his or her ideas on how to create wealth. His or her eyes will be open to seeing what can be done with the available knowledge that has to be acquired as a means to an end-the end being wealth creation. In fact Robert Kiyosaki in his book The Business of the 21st Century has argued out that wealth creation does not take a good formal education to make money. He points out that a college education is important for traditional professions but not for people who want to build wealth. He also puts out that making money does not take money to make money as some people have said.

CHAPTER 6: HIGHLIGHTS ON MY REPOSITIONING MYSELF AND MY FAMILY TO HAVING EMPLOYER MINDS

In order to make sure that what we are sharing is not abstract, I would like to start by sharing with you my personal persuasion leading to this teaching. *Since 2012, I embarked on a repositioning journey which I thought did not need to be travelled alone but with others and in particular my family.* Before fully involving my family, I started by engaging three brothers in the Lord and we made some strides but at a given point they were no longer available. *I however did not give up my resolution to reposition myself to have an employer mind and put the ideas into practice.*

One day after listening to Pastor Sam Adeyemi, on his programme Success Power, on KICC Television, who undertook some stocktaking of what he had, I sat down and did likewise. I carried out stocktaking of what I had both tangible and intangible resources. *I realized that I was the first human capital, then my wife was second and my children in the home were third category of human capital in my home. I also realized that my home was the first arena for me to practice the ideas I had.* In the same year, *I told my family that I wanted to quit my job so that I could pursue the dream I had. That day when I shared the idea to my family was like I had told them that I was about to die.* The first question I was asked was how we were going to survive. This looks to be a normal question in life and somehow it is a fundamental question whose answer limits us from taking risks and living the lives we desire to live. I told them that I was going to translate the ideas I had to make money for a living. Above all I wanted was *to do something that would give me satisfaction and meaning in my life.*

I had reached a level where within me something was telling me that I had potential to do more than I was doing. That day my family put across the usual logical arguments that keep us being employees forever in the name of security instead of enjoying the freedom that an employer has. They argued that I needed to prepare by at least having a source of income to sustain the family. A few people I shared the idea with reacted in a similar manner and they chose to 'counsel me'. Even though I did not quit that time, I have ever since been preparing for my exit from my employer. I then decided to embark on the journey of repositioning my mind to having an employer in me.

The preparation I embarked on ever since had to deal more with my personal development to enable me create value to take to the market as an employer rather than an employee before and after my exit from my employer. I decided to embark on personal development and repositioning my mind and the minds of my family members to have employer minds. In the process the retirement age was pushed to sixty five years of age and I resolved that I would not afford to go to sixty five years as an employee. It meant that I was going to resign because I did not see myself going that far. *At that time I had already started the writings on The Employer in You and I was able to see clearly the employer's behaviour.* I prayed for a change and I thank God they revised the Retirement Age to include fifty Five years requiring that one had to apply one year before the date of expected retirement. At the time of this writing, I am counting months *to exit and be free from the captivity of my employer for twenty seven years at the time I intend to retire at fifty five.* To me that will be being released from the employee captivity I have been held in for many years. *What a day that it will be to be freed from the employer who has held me captive for years!*

REPOSITIONING MYSELF TO EMBARK ON VALUE ADDITION ON MYSELF (PERSONAL DEVELOPMENT) AND CREATING VALUE FOR OTHERS

One of my preparation has been value addition on myself so that I can add value to society that surpasses being an employee. In adding value to myself, I have been studying. This time not studying for promotion. Instead it has been personal development. In so doing, I have written this book entitled: The Employer in You which is in series. I have so far composed over 50 gospel songs and two of the songs are in my daughter Jireh's Album. I have also produced an album for nine of the songs.

For many of us we invested into education as a form of value addition so that we could later *sell our value for a salary instead of using it to produce our own products and have control over them.* This is the main reason for schooling for many people and yet *the reason for going to school to enhance your capacity to be an employer is the best.* What makes it the best is the fact that *the one who decides to be an employer will sell his or her value for a dividend and enjoy the freedom that every employer enjoys.*

TEACHING MY FAMILY TO REPOSITION THEMSELVES TOWARDS HAVING EMPLOYER MINDS

Since 2012 when these insights that I am sharing got more internalized in me than ever before, I have been persuading my children to go to school not thinking of being employees but that they work towards becoming employers. My heart's desire is that they utilize the knowledge from school to become employers and employ those who cannot think for themselves. I have told them that *it does not pay much to spend time acquiring all the degrees, like I have done during my working career, and use them to make another person rich instead of making riches for myself.* If they do not take the path of an entrepreneur whom I am calling an employer, they will have no one to blame since they have got the truth. As I have already stated, *personally I have concluded that it is not too late for me to demonstrate that I can be an employer before I go to the grave.* With Ecclesiastes9:10, in mind, *I have found something to do even though I have done so when I am over fifty three years.* Since I have found something to do, I have to do it with all my might since there is no working, no planning, no wisdom and no knowledge in the grave where I am going. The time to work out my ideas is now. *The time to plan, going forward, with what I have to do is now. The time for me to apply wisdom and knowledge on what I have found to do is now.*

SOME HIGHLIGHTS OF WHAT I HAVE DONE WITH SOME OF MY FAMILY MEMBERS ON REPOSITIONING THEMSELVES TO HAVING EMPLOYER MINDS

WHY EXAMPLES FROM MY FAMILY?

These examples are for me to share with you the extent to which I have been committed to the fact that there is an employer in each one of us. In making the message not simply theory, I ventured into taking some actions that can lead to one being an employer. *I realized that the best place to practice my ideas before sharing with the world was to share them with my family. To me, my home is a power house of ideas and a laboratory.* After testing the employer ideas within my home, we have reached a point where we can share our experience with others like you. *These experiences are a demonstration of the first steps which if fully developed can make one become an employer. The initial steps in transforming yourself into an employer is by you first putting value in yourself and coming up with a product or service to sell to the market.*

MY FAMILY BEING THE FIRST TO BE COMMUNICATED TO REGARDING REPOSITIONING

Since 2012 to date, *I have been communicating to my family that there is an employer in each one of them. The only enemy to them being employers is their minds.* I have personally demonstrated to my family that all things are possible to him who believes. There are a number of things my children told me can't be done but I told them it can. *I either forced them to do something or I did it myself as a demonstration.* One of them is when they told me that they could not design video clips. They told me that videos are designed by experts. I told them that while that was true, *they needed to start from being* amateurs to when they will be professionals or experts in a given field. *I told then that in sports you don't start by being a professional player but you start as an amateur.* With this they designed Jireh's Gospel video and we used the family camera I bought to come up with the videos ourselves with some knowledge from experts.

SHARING OUR EXPERIENCE ON REPOSITIONING OUR MINDS WITH OTHERS

One day I heard one man of God Pastor Sam Adeyemie saying that we need to share our experiences with others. He said that *no matter how small the experience may be, there can be something that can enrich another person's life somewhere.* As already pointed out these insights are a result of our experience as a family and the result of my study of scripture and my experiences during my working career as an employee. They have culminated into: The Employer in You: Repositioning Yourself from having an employee mind to having an Employer Mind and the other series. *This story as I have already pointed out is intended for the whole world as is my prayer to God in one of my recorded songs entitled: Enlarge My Territory, O Lord.* It is a prayer to God that *He enlarges my territory so that my influence may be global since I have come to believe that I am a global marketer.* And you may be part of that audience who may need to listen to this message to bring transformation in your life as regards being an employer.

The following are some of the testimonials regarding the Employer in You as applied in my family:

THE REPOSITIONING STEPS TO MAKE MY DAUGHTER SEE THE EMPLOYER IN HER: JIREH'S COMPLETION OF GRADE 12 AND THE REPOSITIONING EXPERIENCE

When my daughter Jireh finished school in 2012, she told me that she wanted to go and work in one of the Super Markets. I told her that I did not want her to go my way. Instead, *I told her to forego the monies that her friends were getting and I requested her to simply be at home and to be dreaming even when awake.* One day she called me and asked me to give her the verse I liked quoting from the Bible. The verse is Psalms 27:13, which talks about seeing the goodness of the Lord in the land of the living. In the evening of that day I asked her what she wanted the verse for. She told me she was composing a song with her cousin Oscar. This is how Jireh's first album came into being. *From that day onwards I become a music advisor, something that I had never done before.* I also went further to compose songs which I was not doing before this time. And later I started singing together with Jireh and the other members of the family. *We are now in the music industry. At the time of this writing, we had not only established a recording studio at home but gone a step further to use the studio and the other facilities we have acquired to multiply our resources and use the media to market our products and services to the world market. This has brought to us as a family a lot of meaning and fulfilment as we impact people around and beyond us. The rest is now history yet to be shared.*

JIREH'S AND KAHINGA'S FREEZITS MACHINE AS A PRACTICAL ACTION ON REPOSITIONING TO HAVING AN EMPLOYER MIND

Currently Jireh and her husband to be, Kahinga, came up with a freezits machine which is in our home. Using this machine, freezits have been made from my house and the products sold to the market. Meanwhile this has been done while Jireh has been studying at University. *Even if this seems to be in a small way, what is key is that if they develop this habit into a bigger venture, they can end up being employers. This is a simple demonstration of what they are capable of doing if only they repositioned themselves with an employer mind.*

THE REPOSITIONING STEPS TO MAKE MY NEPHEW SEE THE EMPLOYER IN HIM: OSCAR TURNS OUT TO BE A MUSIC PRODUCER AND GOSPEL ARTIST

My nephew Oscar is now able to produce music, as a music producer, which he has never done before. *I persuaded him that there was potential in him to do something he has never dreamed of doing.* Although at the beginning he saw it to be a difficult thing especially with no formal training in music, he is now a music producer. My first Gospel Album got produced by him. Of course when you listen to it carefully, you will notice some mistakes. *But for me the issue is not the mistakes but the fact that something has been done.* We are actually improving the product. *The point is that we have a starting point and are moving from imperfection to perfection* (2Corinthians13:11). Remember that God in Genesis1:1-2, God's creation of the earth started with an earth that was formless, empty and full of darkness. *God then using His Spirit and creative power embarked on a project to bring light, form to the and populated the earth with things until in Genesis 1:31, He looked at all He had made and behold it was very good.* This tells us how we can also create and make things-*move from imperfection to perfection*.

As for my family, where did we start from? It started when we went into music which started with Jireh's Album. We realized that we needed to have our own studio equipment. After getting our studio equipment, we tried to bring in those who knew how to record so as to teach him but the experience was that none of them went to the end. *I encouraged him to move on and finally he produced my first Gospel Album ever and him as his first production ever.* Further, I convinced him that he was capable of being a gospel artist as well. He was reluctant at first but later he realized that he was capable of being a gospel artist. *At the time of this writing, he has produced his first album as a producer and a singer. I have been the advisor to him regarding the songs. This has been very fulfilling on my part.*

THE REPOSITIONING STEPS TO MAKE MY NEPHEW SEE AN EMPLOYER IN HIM: CLEMENT TURNS OUT TO BE A VIDEO PRODUCER

When I was in Bali Indonesia in December, 2012, I decided to buy a camera so that we could use it in coming up with videos. Just like Jesus was able to tell Peter and his brother and friends that they were to be fishers of men, I gave my other nephew the camera and told him that he was to be a camera man. *He then started learning by trial and error and as I am writing this book, he is able to photograph and edit videos. Seven of Jireh's first Gospel Video Album was done by Clement under my guidance. The sense of fulfilment was so enormous that it encouraged me to do more.*

THE OUTCOME OF MY REPOSITIONING: MY BECOMING A SELF MADE GOSPEL ARTIST

After my daughter Jireh had produced her first album with my involvement as an advisor, *I made up my mind to sing as well*. Actually long before she started singing I had composed a song from 2 Chronicles 5:20 entitled Baal Perazim meaning the Lord has broken through my enemies like the breakthrough of waters. This happened while I was of studying the Book of 2 Samuel from Chapter one to chapter nine. *From my bedroom I sang the song at the sitting room and my family members laughed. I, however, did not give up. I went and sang the song at the Men's fellowship and they enjoyed the song. Then I got encouraged that I could then take the singing forward.*

One day after Jireh had produced her Album in which she sang two of the songs I wrote, *I told some of my family members that I wanted to start singing. That night they told me that with my voice I could not sing. They advised that I just write and then they sing. Since I had already made up my mind, I told them that I would go ahead to sing. I further told them if no one liked my songs I would behave like God and like them myself.* I told them that God did not look for approval from anyone before he commended His products. He Himself labelled His products as good until he finally labelled all His creation as very good. This discussion made me put in my best until I travelled with the children to Mongu Town, in Zambia where I went to preach. We then sang together. As we were driving back home I asked them like Jesus asked His disciples about whom they thought He was. *Jireh told me, "Dad from today you are a gospel artist. I will be inviting you to my singing occasions"* Oscar told me, "Uncle you have shocked me today with *your singing."* From that day onwards Jireh started engaging me in her singing invitations and I sung with her. *Now I am singing to the glory of God. What a sense of fulfilment on my part as I see myself living fully and dying empty!*

A LESSON FROM DR DAVID NAMA-OWNER OF DANA SERVICES WHO REPOSITIONED HIMSELF FROM BEING AN EMPLOYEE TO BEING AN EMPLOYER TODAY

On 16th August, 2012, I was privileged to listen to Dr Nama, a businessman, as he spoke to us on how he became a successful entrepreneur. This was during a Doctorate Lecture on Global issues in Entrepreneurship where he was invited as a guest speaker and I was one of the students. *What I learnt from all his sharing was that he repositioned himself from being an employee of a named company to being an employer.* I asked him a question about where some of us would start from in order to be like him? His answer was, " *Start from the idea you have. Your idea could be your competitive advantage. Look for people with the similar idea like yours and learn from them.*" He said he was available to offer advice. What I heard from him was that he walked out of his former workplace without resigning. That was the end of him being an employee. *Like Jacob, who walked away from Laban's company, Dr Nama walked away from his former workplace. The story about his success as an employer, as I listened to him, was anchored on his walking out of his former workplace.* The surprising thing is that he was working in a reputed company which most of us would find it difficult to leave the way he did. *Surely he should have repositioned himself from having an employee mind to having an employer mind.*

Dr Nama talked about aiming to employ 1000 employees from over 200 that he had that time. He talked of him sitting down while making money. He had reached a level of consolidating his wealth. He reminded me of God resting on the seventh day admiring his creation. As he talked he reminded me of the Late Dr. Myles Munroe who shared on the application of the four business laws namely being fruitful, multiplying the fruit, distributing the fruit and subduing with your fruit. *What went on in my mind was that Dr. Nama had become fruitful, multiplied his fruit, distributed it, and subdued in a particular area in society and now he had dominated in that area. He was now an employer. He like Jacob had transformed himself from having an employee mind to having an employer mind. Ultimately he became an employer at last.* Interesting enough, I was among the Doctorate students who were eager to stand by his side to have a photo with him. He was a prosperous man worth having a photo with. *I was among those who admired a man who behaved differently from me and made a difference in his life.*

What I learned from that day onwards was that *the start of our success borders on the way we act on that good idea that is in our spirit, the idea that is in our mind. We need to create something and make something out of our creation. Now how did it begin* with Dr. Nama or with Jacob or any other person who transformed himself or herself? *How did it begin* with people like Mr. Les Brown and the Jim Rohn who have influenced the world with their gifts? This is the big question. *It began by them repositioning themselves from having employee minds to having employer mind. Dr. Nama, like Jacob, Jim Rohn and Les Brown and others who made a difference, repositioned himself from implementing another person's idea to implementing their own ideas.* I take it that they took calculated risks by resolving like Caleb and Joshua that they were giants who were able to breakthrough and not like grasshoppers. *They undertook stock taking of what God had put in them and started thinking like a rich men and worked towards making the ideas they had into reality no matter what.* They, like Moses, forsook the treasures of Egypt (Hebrews 11:27) because they saw the invisible. *They forsook the treasures of the comfort zones in which they were before they ventured into what they ended up becoming.*

How many of us would walk out of our workplaces and go on the street thinking that one day we will be rich? For many of us this would look impossible. Yet *the start of our success borders on the way we act on those good ideas that drop into our minds.*

WHY SHOULD YOU REPOSITION YOUR MIND?

Repositioning your mind is the key to transformation. That is why you need to reposition your mind so that you can experience transformation in your life. For you to realize the employer in you, there is need for repositioning to take place in your mind. *Repositioning your mind has to do with having a paradigm (model, pattern, standard) shift.* It is about change in the positioning of your mind after deciding not to conform to the patterns of this world. This requires having a different spirit like that of Caleb in the Bible (Numbers 14:26).

In what position have you placed your mind? It needs to be repositioned if you expect different results. The Apostle Paul calls it mind renewal. He says that *first don't be conformed to the world's patterns and then be transformed by renewing your mind so that you can test the good, pleasing and accepted will of God* (Romans 12:2). The Sociologist Auguste Committee calls it *change in type of thinking which leads to social change.* According to Bob Proctor *there are what are called paradigms and these paradigm control your life, your income and everything.* He calls *the paradigm as a terror barrier which prevents you from doing what you know you are supposed to do.* Paradigm holds you where you are. *When your paradigm shifts you have a breakthrough in your life. It makes you have a shift in your mind and your actions follow suit and that makes you have a big change in your life. It all starts with a paradigm shift which is repositioning your mind.*

It is paradigm shift which made Jacob change his economic situation within the same environment in a period of about six years which he was not able to do in fourteen years. *The man who only depended on wages for over fourteen years changed his economic status within a shorter period to become wealthy and owned camels, donkeys, flocks, female servants and male servants. This breakthrough came as a result of breaking the paradigm and decided to move in the direction that changed his economic situation.*

Repositioning your mind and deciding to move in a particular direction will help you to live the life you have imagined. Henry David Thoreau pointed out that:

> "If a person will advance confidently in the direction of their dream and endeavour to live the life they have imagined, they will meet with success unexpected in common hours."

Repositioning your mind will make you start moving in a direction that will make you meet with success unexpected in common hours.

REPOSITIONING YOURSELF TO BEING A CORPORATE ENTREPRENEUR IF YOU ARE EMPLOYED

According to Wolcott and Lippitz on www.seipa.edu.pl, they define the term corporate entrepreneurship as a process by which teams within an established company conceive, foster, launch and manage a new business that is distinct from the parent company but leverages the parent company's assets, market positions, capabilities or other resources. In this regard, *corporate entrepreneurs are employed in corporations but they have an entrepreneurial mind and are business partners who may be shareholders in the business*. They might be drawing a salary from a corporation for the work they do but at the same time they may be shareholders of the company. *These have transformed themselves beyond employees to being employee-employers. They may have an aim of finally being on their own as employers with having employed employees to think for them.*

This is what Jacob did. He made himself a corporate entrepreneur as he took advantage of being in Laban's enterprise and came up with innovation that led to growth in his wealth even though he was still working for Laban. He leveraged on the resources in Laban's enterprise and made his fortune out of it. Of course he did not steal but did things legally by agreeing with Laban on the terms of engagement. They entered into a business contract that saw Jacob become an employer in the long run. *Jacob is a good example of a corporate entrepreneur to emulate by those currently in corporations.*

According to Napoleon Hill, in his Book entitled the Master Key to Riches he points out that *every man who works for a wage or salary should recognize and respect one key fact. This is the fact that his job is and should be a schooling for a higher station in life.* To him you are being paid in two important ways at your work place. The first way of payment is by the wages you receive directly from your work. The second payment is by the experience you gain from your work. To him he says that *it becomes true that a man's greatest pay consists not in his pay envelope but in the experience he gains from his work.*

So *the point here is that if you are working, your greatest pay is the experience you gain from your work. This is what Jacob capitalized on while working for Laban.* He then used the acquired experience to acquire wealth for himself as can be seen in Genesis30:43.

THE GUEST HOUSE WITH FIVE SELF CONTAINED ROOMS

In July, 2017 I sat in a meeting with my family members as we were preparing to open a Guest House with five self-contained rooms. The meeting was chaired by my nephew who assumed the role of manager and as my wife and I participated in the deliberations, I saw the beauty of being an employer. I felt fulfilled having taken years to bring the Guest House to the level we expected for it to bring us revenue. *What I got excited with most was the way my family members contributed their minds into planning for the future of the business.* At a given point I was asked a question similar to the one Peter asked Jesus Christ in the Bible in Matthew19:27-30 as to what was there for them in terms of returns. *I asked if Peter was on a pay or he was a shareholder in Jesus' business. I told them that though it is silent, Jesus' response did not show immediate gratification regarding the hundred fold return to them in this life but futuristic after they had invested themselves into the business.* Further, my response was that they were to choose between being employees to get a wage and being shareholders in the returns from the guesthouse. So *the issue for each one of us is how our expectations are supposed to be met. Should we be paid wages or we should have dividends declared to us? How you position yourself matters when it comes to having your expectations met.*

CHAPTER 7: THE POWER OF THE MIND IN REPOSITIONING YOURSELF

THE POWER OF THE MIND IN PRODUCT DEVELOPMENT

The mind has the capacity to imagine big things. It can think big and end up bringing big results. As the mind acts as a dropbox in which ideas drop, it has the power to imagine big things. *A number of the inventions we have seen and those yet to be invented are a product of the mind.* Literature has attested to the power of the mind. Literature has also established that the mind is so powerful that it determines what you actually become. *That is why whoever wants to control you will start by influencing your mind. The moment your mind changes your actions will follow suit. The employer in you is about your mind- unlocking your potential so that you can imagine all you can be in this earth. For you to make a difference, you need to cultivate the mind of an employer within you.* Professor Peter Shepherd, in his book The Leadership Mind has talked about the importance of the type of mind that one has. *The type of mind you have determines how you behave and the outcome of your life.*

THE MIND AS THE DROPBOX

There is what is being called dropbox in the internet world. *Our minds/hearts are like dropboxes. In Genesis 31:10-12, Jacob testifies that he had a dream in which he saw animals mating and that the Angel of God spoke to him. God dropped an idea into Jacob's mind in a dream.* When he woke up, *he looked into the dropbox, the mind, for the idea which God dropped into his mind*. Jacob implemented the idea by putting sticks where the animals were mating. *What was dropped into the dropbox of Jacob was the output, the three colors. With the output in mind, the other idea of the sticks the resources to be used to have the three colors were also dropped into his dropbox.* Ultimately as indicated in Genesis 30:37-39, Jacob did exactly what God showed him and the result is what we see in Genesis 30:43. Jacob was transformed from being an employee, a wage earner, to being a wealthy man in terms of the assets he had acquired. The secret for Jacob was with the dropbox-his mind. *The secret for your success is in your dropbox-your mind*.

GOD PUTS THE THING, THE IDEA, THE SUBSTANCE INTO YOUR MIND.

What God drops into our "dropboxes" called minds is not for decoration. **He wants outputs to come out of your "Dropbox", your mind.** For example in 1Chronicles28:2 we learn that King David had it in his heart (his mind) to build a temple for the LORD. It is this thought that led David to come up with a plan to build the Temple though God told him that it was his son to do it. *It starts with the idea. You move the idea from the invisible realm into the visible realm by coming up with a plan for implementing what has been dropped into your mind.* Then you come up with what Tony Robbins calls massive action plan to put the plan into action and come up with the intended results.

THE POWER OF IMAGINATION

Let us consider the following quotes on imagination and apply them to our discussion:

> "Imagination is more important than knowledge. For knowledge is limited, whereas imagination embraces the entire world, stimulating progress, giving birth to evolution." Albert Einstein

> "Logic will take you from A to B, imagination will take you everywhere." Albert Einstein

> "The true sign of intelligence is not knowledge but imagination." Albert Einstein

As can be seen from the quotations from Albert Einstein, *imagination is very important in making us embrace the world.* While on a study tour in Chongqing, one of the biggest cities in China, I saw a write-up on one of the shops saying *the world is my runway*. I saw this to be interesting and tried to see the type of imagination in the mind of the one who came up with the write up. I thought that the person who devised such a write up could have had in mind the idea that before flying into the sky, to enjoy the beauty of travelling to other places, the world acts as a runway. *We are like an aeroplane at the airport which uses a runway in preparing for takeoff as well as for landing.* Given the world as our runway, we too use it in preparing for our takeoff and also for landing at the imagined destination. *In order to move to other places where we get what we desire to get, you start with imagination. Imagination can take us anywhere.*

Imagination can lead you into creation of things in your mind which you can translate into tangible things. The Bible in Jeremiah6:19 talks about *the fruit of your thoughts. So it means that your mind or your thoughts as you imagine can produce a fruit and that fruit can be made tangible when it is translated into a tangible product or service. It all starts with your mind. It starts with your imagination.* Of course the type of imagination matters. The type of imagination determines the type of product and services you produce.1

Chronicles29: talks about imagination of the thoughts of your heart bring drawn to God so that you can produce results.

PEOPLE WHO USED THER MINDS TO IMAGINE

The power of imagination can be seen at babel in Genesis 11. They imagined putting up a tower to heaven and they were determined to do saw. *God saw that what they had imagined to do would not fail* unless they were disturbed.

Look at Jacob's imagination: Getting the colors he wanted (Genesis 30:37-39). In Genesis31:10-13, we see that Jacob started with the dream in which he saw that the animals that mated gave three colors stripped, spotted and mottled. The Angel told Jacob to lift up his eyes and see that all the goats that mate with the flocks were stripped, spotted and mottled. As we have already alluded to, God through the angel told Jacob the reason why He had intervened. He said that He had seen all that Laban was doing to him. *Jacob then implemented his dream and went into product development.* The results of the power of imagination are recorded in Genesis 30:43. *It is Jacob's imagination that was combined with the dream revealed to him by God and acting that led to his amassing wealth from Laban's enterprise.*

Another man who used his mind to imagine was Abraham. When God took Abraham outside to see the stars in the universe, he wanted Abraham to have a vision by first imagining how many stars were in the universe. The question from God could have been: Abraham can you count the stars? Abraham could have thought in his mind that he could not count them all. He could have responded that he could not manage to count the stars. Then God said if you can't count the stars because they are too many to count, this is how your descendants will be. This resulted in God changing his name from Abram to Abraham. Abraham went through a lot of imagination for him to actualize what God had brought out from his mind. Also when Abraham parted company with Lot, God told him to look north, south, east and west and that what he saw would be his. This is still a teaching on Abraham going into the process of imagination. *What he saw in his mind was going to be his if he arose and walked in the length and breadth of the land. Abraham did what God told him to do and Genesis24:1 says that God blessed Abraham in all things. This is where the secret for being blessed in all things lies.*

The woman with the issue of blood is also another example of people who imagined and made what they imagined come into being (Mark 5:24-34). *I one time gave a teaching on this which I entitled changing gears. This woman changed gears of her mind from say gear one to gear five and accelerated into the realm of faith and got her healing after wasting a lot of resources on doctors. She thought/she said in her mind/she imagined in her mind being healed by Jesus if only she took a step to touch the hem of Jesus' garment.* This she did and got healed. *This is the power of imagination. It can make the invisible become visible; the intangible be tangible.*

THE POWER OF IMAGINATION: THE EMPLOYER'S DISTINCTIVE COMPETENCE

An employer has better imagination than an employee. While an employee imagines getting educated and being employed and having a good job, the employer imagines employing those who would make money for him. Each one of them ends up getting the product of their type of imagination. This is the way our minds have been fashioned. *What you imagine becoming, you increase the chances of having it or becoming it.*

IMAGINE YOU HAVING THE CREATOR'S MIND IN YOU –YOU HAVE THE MIND OF CHRIST

We are told in 1Corinthians2:16 that we have the mind of Christ. You know that Christ is the creator of all things visible and invisible and this is the one whose mind is in you and me! *Just imagine you and I having the mind of Christ, the one who is the architect and builder of all creation!* The creator is in your mind and my mind meaning that you and I have the capacity to think and plan things that can demonstrate that you have the mind of Christ. 1 Corinthians1:30 says that Christ has become our wisdom. *Just imagine the Creator being your wisdom. Just imagine, the one who used wisdom to build the earth and used understanding to establish the heavens and the one who used knowledge to drop due to the earth and populate the earth with precious things, resides in you and me.* You and I can do great things because as He is so are we in this world (1John4:17). *He who was able to pay taxes by getting money from the belly of fish and who was able to feed thousands with two fish and five loaves of bread resides in you. You then can do wonders if we become employers or are already employer.*

ALL TREASURES OF WISDOM AND KNOWLEDGE ARE HIDDEN IN CHRIST; HENCE THE TREASURES ARE IN YOU.

The Bible in Colosians2:3 says that *all the treasures of wisdom and knowledge are hidden in Christ.* Now Colossians 1:27, says that there is a mystery that Christ in you the hope of Christ. So if Christ is in you, then it means that *in you is hidden the treasures of wisdom and knowledge. What then you and I need to do is to mine the treasures of wisdom and knowledge in us resulting from Christ being in us.* This then reminds me of what James1:5 says. James says that if you lack wisdom ask for wisdom. He is not saying that you lack wisdom. He assumes that you have wisdom because 1

Corinthians1:30, says that Christ has become wisdom for you and me. What he is saying is that in case you realize that you lack wisdom, then ask. *The point is that treasures of wisdom and knowledge are hidden in you and me. So we need to mine this treasure and use it to create products and services for us to market to the world as global marketers.*

THE POWER OF AN IDEA IN YOUR MIND

The idea in your mind is like a seed that can produce fruit in your life. As already pointed out in this Book, *your mind is like a drop box in which God drops ideas. The mind can be able to imagine big things and can be able to move thousands of kilometres to places where the body has not been. Your mind has the capacity to see markets in places where the body has not been and start imagining the products and services to be made.* It has been said that the mind is one of the most powerful gifts God has given to each one of us. The mind has the capacity to produce the fruit we require to take to the market. Use that idea in your mind and act on it to bring transformation in your life.

WHO ARE YOU THINKING FOR? THINKING FOR YOURSELF OR YOUR EMPLOYER?

You are either thinking for yourself or for your employer. Many in the world think more for the employers than they think for themselves. *I have been one of the culprits of thinking for the employer more than I have thought for myself and my family.* What do I mean? During my working career for my employer for over twenty five years, I have spent most of my time at the workplace. Each day except for weekends and holidays has been spent for the employer. The workplace is designed for you and me to spend those hours for the employer. What this means is that, as an employee, most of your thinking is for the employer's interest than for yourself. You spend most of the time thinking how to bring out the products and services that the employer wants in exchange for a wage. In a way *my mind got sold up to the employer just as my time had been sold to him when I entered into an employment contract. Had I not entered into an employment contract, I was going to have hundred percent of my time in my control.* This means that thinking for myself was going to be allocated hundred percent. *I believe that it is at this point who you are thinking for that the difference in wealth acquisition starts.*

Thinking for yourself hundred percent is the starting point for wealth creation for yourself. Instead of creating wealth for an employer, you spend your hundred percent time to create your own wealth. It is allocation of hundred percent of your work thought towards wealth creation which leads to wealth acquisition making you a wealth person. Though Jacob continued working for Laban after repositioning himself in his mind, he had in a way moved from thinking for Laban but was thinking about Himself as a partner in the business with Laban. *Remember that there relations had changed from employee- employer to employer- employer relations as business partners.* As we have already established, Jacob had transformed himself to what are nowadays being called corporate entrepreneurs.

MIND RENEWAL KEY IN BECOMING AN EMPLOYER

As we have already pointed out above, mind renewal is key in bringing about transformation in our lives. That is why the Bible tells us in Romans12:2 that the pre-requisite for testing the good, acceptable and perfect will of God is mind renewal. But as we have earlier stated, mind renewal takes place when we choose not to conform to the patterns of this world in which we find ourselves. *The day you will change your mind about something that is the day things will start change in your life.* This change of mind can either be in the negative or in the positive sense.

For Jacob to have brought about transformation in his life in a positive manner from barely surviving when he had an employee mind to becoming rich, he had first to renew his mind. Like we have pointed out already, you see it from the fact that after working for over fourteen years for his uncle as a good manager but had nothing to talk about except his two wives and the thirteen children (Genesis 30:25-27). *Jacob reasoned in his mind that despite him being a good manager in Laban's enterprise, the fruit of his good management was reaped by his employer Laban.*

Interesting enough Laban himself confessed that the LORD had blessed him because of Jacob. Laban was rich but Jacob was poor despite his hard work. *Laban had the mind to think in an employer way which resulted in riches while Jacob thought the employee way which resulted in poverty.* It was not until he went through what I call mind renewal that he found the secret. *The secret lay in who owned the means of production.* He could have realized that the side where you are in your mind determines the side you will find yourself as regards riches. *Jacob was on the employee side in his mind and ended up reaping what he had sown-a wage which is the payment for the sown labour. Laban on the other hand had to reap profits leading to dividends which are the reaping from the sown seed called capital.* What type of seed are you going to sow? *Is it labour or capital you are sowing or are going to sow?*

I believe *Jacob learned a hard lesson to realize, like I have realized as well, that he had undervalued himself.* As a result he got peanuts out of the transaction. As we have established already, instead of benefiting from the dividends in a balance sheet, Jacob was paid from the cost of production. So he was a "cost" in as far as expenses on the side of the employer were concerned. Despite him being perceived by Laban to be an "asset" in terms of being human capital from the perspective of Laban, Jacob was actually a liability when it came to expenses to be incurred by Laban. So it was more helpful for Laban, like many employers would do, to pay Jacob Peanuts so that by minimizing costs he would maximize profits. As we have established, Jacob's mind renewal led to him changing his status quo. He had to take steps to move in the direction of his new ideas.

THE DIFFERENCE BETWEEN AN EMPLOYER MIND AND AN EMPLOYEE MIND

I know of a practical example of *the difference between an employer mind and an employee mind.* Some people met at a point where they were doing the same course with one who was already running an organization as an employer. They on the other hand were employees where they came from. At the end of the course they all got similar qualifications. *One would expect that these who were employees would at this point transform themselves into employers and for example partner with the colleague who was already an employer.* Interesting enough one of the courses they all did was Entrepreneurship. After completing the course the one who was already an employer ended up employing into his organization those who were already employees. They could have most likely got better salaries compared to where they came from, better titles and better conditions. But *the one who was an employer did not get them to pay them for nothing. He wanted to pay them in order for them to increase his returns to his investment.*

Where was the difference since they all equalized in terms of qualification and may be those employed could have been more knowledgeable than the employer? *The difference was in perspective. It is in the way the employer mind thinks compared to the employee mind. The employer mind goes to read in order to employ those who know how to think and the employee mind goes to read in order to be employed by the employer who knows why he/she should think.*

In a nutshell, the difference between an employee and an employer is as follows:

- Knowing how to think verses knowing why you should think

- Having different mind-sets (Culture)
- One is a risk taker and the other is risk averse (opposed, antagonistic)
- One is a long term perspective thinker (the employer) while the other (the employee) is more interested in the short and medium term.

AN EMPLOYEE AS AN ASSET ON ONE HAND AND A LIABILITY ON THE OTHER HAND

When looked at as a cost of production, an employee is a liability to an organization. When looked at as human capital, an employee becomes an asset to the organization. For Jacob, just like for many of us who are employees, *Laban had two perspectives about him. When Laban looked at Jacob in terms of the turnaround and the business growth he had experienced, Jacob was an asset.* This can be seen to the extent that he willing to change the employment arrangement in order to prevent him from leaving. *When Laban looked at Jacob from the reward side, Jacob became a liability.*

WHAT TYPE OF REPORT HAS YOUR MIND WRITTEN AND PRODUCED

In the Bible in Numbers13, God told Moses to send 12 leaders into the Promised Land to spy the land that they were destined to possess with God's help. They went into that land and took forty days to spy the land. Finally, they were required to give a report of what they had seen. The report presented was quite interesting. *At the opening of the Report, all the twelve agreed that the land was very good and they even presented tangible evidence in form of fruit which they brought from that land. The contrast among the two groups that emerged came on the conclusion of the report.*

The 10 out of 12 Reporters said that they had seen themselves in their own eyes like grasshoppers and also in the eyes of the giants they were as grasshoppers. As such their final position was that they were not able to go and possess the land. *In contrast, Caleb and Joshua acknowledged the giants that they saw but they saw themselves as giants because they had God beside them.* They then disagreed with them and concluded that they were well able to possess the land. What we learn from this is that *each person writes a report on the mind from which positions are taken and then speech is made from such a report from the mind.* Sometimes this report can be written down but it is the fruit of the mind. *The type of reports each wrote on their minds made a difference in the conclusions and decisions they made and the direction they took going forward.*

Relating this to the Employer in You insights, *the report you create in your mind as to whether you can be an employee or employer makes a difference. What you have experienced; what you have seen; what you have heard; what you have been told and other things makes you come up with a report in your mind.* There are at least two categories of report writers in the employment discussion. On one hand, these experiences can make you create *and write a report in your mind which reads "I am unable to be an employer"*. There are on the other hand those who translate their experiences of what they have heard; seen and been told and have seen themselves capable of being employers and *write a report, "I am well able to be an employer".*

DEPLOYMENT MAKES A DIFFERENCE

You either deploy yourself in your mind as an employee or deploy yourself to be an employer. God deployed us on earth to be employers but many of us redeployed ourselves to be employees. There is already a gene of an employer in you and me. We see this in Jacob when he decided to have a shift in his paradigm. *The change in his thinking transformed him from Genesis30:25-26 case to Genesis30:43 case.*

YOU ARE TOO LOADED TO WAIT FOR THINGS TO HAPPEN- REMOVE THE EMPLOYEE THINKING AND BEHAVIOUR TO HAVE AN EMPLOYER BEHAVIOUR

I recently listened to one man of God whose name I cannot remember saying:

- You are too loaded to wait for things to happen
- You cannot stay with no venture and no investment
- What you need as the last step to make things happen is courage
- God wants to partner with you.
- What makes a lion is its heart. It is its attitude that makes a difference.

Having listened to the man of God, I took it personal that I was too loaded to be among those who wait for things to happen. I realized that I had what it takes to change situations through my initiatives. What I needed was to partner with God as I developed an attitude like that of a lion. Actually I have the Lion of the Tribe of Judah in me. What will make you and I to be employers are our hearts. It is your type of attitude and my type of attitude that will make a difference. *It is your type of mind and my type of mind that will make a difference as to whether we are employees or employers.*

SOME QUESTIONS AND ANSWERS TO CONSIDER ON THE TWO TYPES OF MINDS: THE EMPLOYEE MIND AND EMPLOYER MIND

The following are some questions and possible answers to consider regarding the two types of minds- the employee mind and the employer mind:

1. Did God give employee or an employer minds to individuals? *God put in all of us employer minds.* Our culture and secular approach have made many of us conformed to employee minds.
2. What is an employee mind and what is an employer mind? An employee mind is a mind that thinks that by offering labour one can receive wages or a salary. *The employer mind is the mind that thinks that by producing products or services using paid for labour of an employee mind, one can get profits and ultimately acquire wealth.*
3. What is the difference between these two types of minds? *The difference between the two is in their perspective* which determines what they finally get from business transaction.
4. *What is the perspective of an employee mind*? To sell his /her labour to get ultimately a wage or a salary including some other conditions of service.
5. *What is the perspective of an employer mind?* It is a mind to invest capital, land, labour and entrepreneurship in order to ultimately get dividends.
6. *Are the outcomes of these minds the same*? The outcomes are obviously different. The outcome is that the employee mind ends up being a servant to the employer mind. *The employer mind takes the day by controlling the employee mind.*
7. *Which type of mind gets the best out of what they put in an enterprise?* The answer is obvious. The employee mind gets wages which are the payment legally for offering labour. *The employer mind gets the best both in benefiting from the profits which rewards him with dividends.*

CHAPTER 8: RELEASING THE EMPLOYER IN YOU

THERE IS ALREADY AN EMPLOYER INSIDE YOU CRYING TO BE RELEASED

You are carrying a "pregnancy" of an employer in you crying out to be birthed out of you. That unborn baby cries inside you struggling to be released from your "womb" but you have always suppressed him. You have failed to deliver your own child because you have been inclined to taking care of "someone's child" for a wage or a salary. This is a choice which you have made or may make and it determines the results you end up getting.

YOU WERE BORN AN EMPLOYER; BORN A BUSINESS PERSON

As we have seen so far God created you as an employer with room also for you to choose to be an employee. Remember in the Garden of Eden, God created man and blessed him to be fruitful, to multiply, to distribute his fruitfulness and to subdue using his fruitfulness and ultimately dominate. God told man to behold what He had given him- plants with seed in them (Genesis1:29-30) and God told man to manage what he had given him. (Genesis2:15). *God gave man business to do on the onset. Each one of us has some business to do whether we are doing it or not.* God put man in the position of an employer from the very beginning. We see it from Adam to Noah. We also see it in Abraham and Isaac. These were employers. They employed servants who were in a sense employees. *Being an employer or an employee then is a choice that you make. You either decide to be a master (an employer) to someone or a servant (an employee) to someone.*

GOD'S VALUATION OF YOU AND ME

Having been made in the image and likeness of God, He has crowned you with glory and honour. You wear a crown of glory and honour. *You are a dignified individual in the sight of God.* So you are not useless but useful in the sight of God. *You are by design not a failure but a success.* You are designed to be wise; to progress and be a success. It does not matter what people call you. What matters most is what label God puts on you. *You are by design not poor but rich because of what God has already given you.* 2 Peter1:3-4 says that God's divine nature has given us all things we need for life and godliness. According to Psalms8:5-6, *God designed you and me for dominion here on earth* (Gensis1:28).*God made you and me managers in charge of the resources he created.* The Bible says God has given the earth to the sons of men. *God has given you and me dominion over the works of his hands.* He has put all things under your feet.

The following is a listing of some of the resources God has put in the earth to qualify you and me to be employers:

- All the sheep and oxen
- The beasts of the fields
- The fish of the sea
- Whatever passes through the paths of the sea.

In Psalms 8:1, David starts with an exclamation on how majestic the name of the Lord is in all the earth. In Psalms 8:9, he concludes with the same. *In between he brings out God's creative power. He talks about what God has put in place in the Heavenly places.* David starts and concludes with God's name. God is name is majestic in all the earth. *He singled out man as unique creation that God is mindful of and cares for more than any to the extent that he gave man His only begotten son.* This man should obviously be valuable in the sight of God. In fact the son of Man Psalms 8 is a prophetic reference to Jesus Christ as the Son of man as indicated in Hebrews2:5-9,

You are of high value in sight of God. For this very reason God made you and me to be in-charge of his creation. In so doing he crowned you with glory and honour. That is why no man has a right to marginalise you. You are dignified in the sight of God. *You need mind renewal regarding this in order to see transformation in yourself and your business. You can see from this that you are by nature an employer with the potential to exploit some of the resources listed above.*

WHAT SHOULD YOU DO WITH THE EMPLOYER POTENTIAL IN YOU?

The Bible in John8:32 says that you shall know the truth and the truth will set you free. In John13:17 Jesus said if you know these things, you are blessed if you do them. *The tone you get from Psalms 8 is that of the creator and the one the creator has put in place to be the man in charge of earth.* It establishes that God is an overall leader who has given man dominion in order for man to have leadership on earth. It points out that man has the following at his disposal:

1. Ownership of the resources in the earth
2. The capacity, which includes brain capacity, to exploit the resources
3. The time to exploit the resources
4. Room to acquire skills to exploit the resources on the earth
5. The capacity to work with one's hands.
6. Opportunity to see the availability of resources and be able to exploit them.

7. God's partnership in the whole equation.

If God created you in his own image, you have the ability to create like God. If you are the son of God you resemble your Father and as such you have the power to create. As quoted above, 1 Corinthians 2:16 says that you have the mind of Christ. ***Every child of God has the creator's mind.*** As a child of God you are not supposed to be stranded even when you find yourself stranded. ***When you are born again there is a mind transplant from Jesus to you. The mind of Christ was transplanted into your mind.*** This then means that you are a thinker like Christ and have the capacity to create as an employer.

THE EMPLOYER IN YOU IS LIKE AN ENCLOSED ENVELOPE WAITING TO BE OPENED AND THE VALUABLE CONTENTS TRANSFORMED INTO VALUABLE PRODUCTS OR SERVICES

At a workshop facilitated by Dr. Gumboh, at which I was a participant and him as a consultant, he shared what he called a philosophy of development. He said that development is like opening an envelope, which has hidden potential. It is sealed with something valuable in us. After hearing what he said, I pondered on the point and saw that ***development has two sides namely the exploitation of the hidden potential and the transformation or change that comes with the exploitation of that hidden potential.*** This then brings us to the dominion mandate in the Bible which introduces the development concept in Gensesis1:28 and Psalms8:4-6 and other verses. ***We see that development is the ultimate for man where the potential endowment in man and the resources around and beyond man are exploited.*** The two secrets to development is for man to:

- behold the seed in him (man's potential) as the blessing God placed in man (Genesis1:28) and

- see the seed in the resources (Genesis1:29) around and beyond where man is (resource potential).

By man being fruitful, he adds value to his own value and adds value to the resources around him and beyond him. This then responds to the demand in the market as portrayed in Genesis8:22. This demand is satisfied by man using the potential in himself/herself and around him/her to add value to the endowed resources that God has given him in the universe. Man then has no excuse for being stranded as far as God is concerned.

DISCOVERING YOURSELF AS AN EMPLOYER

Many of us were brought up and taught that we were born to be employees. We ended up with an understanding that we needed to go to school solely for a purpose of being employed. Very few were taught otherwise. A few were never taught but they used intuition to go on the employer side. Others were forced to take the employer route after failing to find employment. But when you start asking yourself some questions and give answers to them, you reach a stage where you see an employer in yourself. Questions like who am I? What kind am I made of? What am I made of and why was I made? *Can I bring forth something as a product or service? What do I have in my hand? What can I do with what is in me and with me? Is there a market for what I can produce? You will discover that there is something you can do to make you an employer.*

As the Late man of God Myles Munroe pointed out in his teachings, *many people live on earth without knowing who they are and what they were born to do and what they can do*. They do not realize that they have giants inside them. *They can only bring out the giants in them when they look inside themselves and bring out what they have stored inside for many years. When you discover who you really are, what staff you are made of and what you can do with it, you look "crazy" to some people.* You feel like flying out like a bird that has been caged for many years but now loosed. *You realize that you have not been doing what you were made to do and feel like you are behind and wanting to do the best you could.*

Recently I met a colleague with whom I was at the university. As we chatted, *I told him that I was leaving one locality to another so that I could do and pursue what I have come up with. He told me, "That is what happens when people discover themselves".* I told him that I was actually writing something connected to discovering yourself as an employer.

DISCOVERING YOURSELF AS AN EMPLOYER IS EQUIVALENT TO FINDING YOUR ORIGINAL PURPOSE REGARDING WORK

When you realize that there is an employer in you, the result is that your thinking changes. This change brings you to the discovery of your original purpose here on earth. *You find your purpose when you discover yourself and know who you are, what you have, what you are able to do and why you are alive up to this moment.* As we have already pointed out, when asking these questions like: who am I? Of what kind am I made of? What can I do? What am I supposed to bring fourth? What am I made of and why was I made? The responses to these questions can make you awaken from your slumber. *Taking time to look for answers to the questions can make you end up being provoked to act in line with the revelations you get from the answers and awaken the employer in you.*

A BETTER TAIL IS ONE YOU GROW ON YOUR OWN (MUKILA WAWUWAHI WAKUDIMENENA EYI AWENI)

"Mukila wawuwahi wakudimenena eyi aweni" is saying in Lunda Language spoken in Zambia and other countries which can be translated to mean that a better tail is one you grow on your own. *The meaning of this is that it is better to have your personal ownership than when you depend on what another person owns.* It is like an animal without a tail borrowing a tail from another. The thinking is that the tail you get from someone is good but your own grown tail is better. *Applied to the Employer in you discussion, you will realize that it pays to be a business owner than being an employee.* With your own, the amount of freedom is more than when you are an employee. It pays to be an employer. *An employer 'grows' his or her own 'tail'.*

EARNING THE BREAD WE EAT

2Thessalonians3: 6-12 tells us not to be idle but to earn the bread we eat. Now what is to earn? When you check the synonyms for To Earn some of them are:

- To make
- To receive
- To get
- To be paid

In the past I used to relate this to being an employee until I realized that it does not say become an employee but it emphasizes working, not a job. *You were born to work since you are not like a bird which does not sow, reap and store in barns.* What the bird cannot do, you have the capacity to. That is why God places high value on you. But what type of work? Is it where you become an employee or an employer? This is the question that this teaching aims to answer. You make a choice as to which side to take. *But this book is bringing out God's original intention for you and me. It also brings out the fact that there is an employer in you yearning to be released in that it is the better side to belong to.*

DISCOVERING YOURSELF IS EQUIVALENT TO KNOWING THE POTENTIAL YOU HAVE

The Man of GOD Myles Munroe said "purpose= potential". Why is it so? He said this because potential is given to us equivalent to the purpose we were created for. After knowing your purpose, you use potential to accomplish that purpose. Potential is untapped ability, untapped power which you were given when you were created to fulfill your purpose. Your purpose becomes your calling which became your ministry or your work. This applies even to your being an employer. *When you look within yourself, you discover that you have employer potential in you if only you dealt with your mind.*

HOW DO YOU DISCOVER YOURSELF AS AN EMPLOYER?

In order to discover yourself as an employer, *you have to listen to that voice that speaks within you and tells you that you have something big. It tells you that you have something worth being consumed on the market.* To begin with, what it means to discover yourself is to start bringing out something that is hidden even in you its raw state. We may not realize that it was there requiring us to give birth to it. As we have already stated, there is a child crying in your womb to be born. *Do not die with the child that God put in you to offer to society.* Again the Man of God Myles Munroe said, *do not rob your generation of that which you should have given to them as an employer.*

You may need to be involved in a search for the things of value in you and exchange them with those that you are currently occupied with. *The parables of the pearl of great value and the hidden treasure are a good illustration on discovering things of greater value and trading what we value for things of greater value.* I remember when I was about nine years old I get involved in hunting with my grandfather. There were times we went to look for animals in the bush but ended up discovering more valuable things than what we were looking for. *The discovery of the valuable things of greater value was as a result of going into the bush. We gave up what was of lower value and got what was of higher value within the same bush.*

The following are some of the points that can help us discover ourselves as employers:

1. *Remember that God the "manufacturer" who created us knows how we really are, what He wired into us and what we can do.* God made Moses discover himself and what he was able to do by telling him to throw a staff he had used for forty years without realizing it would be transformed into a snake (Exodus4:1-4). *God knew the potential Moses was carrying for years without utilizing it for things of high*

value. There is potential in you that you could be misusing or underutilizing. He also made Jeremiah discover himself by reminding him that he was known while in his mother's womb. Jeremiah was told that what he required was self-assertiveness and swinging into action (Jeremiah 1:5).

2. *There is a voice in each one of us which tells us that there is something we can do beyond what have so far done in our lives and another voice that tells us we cannot do it.* To discover ourselves, we need to pay much more attention to the voice which says we can do it and ignore the one that tells us that we can't.

3. *Jesus discovered himself in scriptures.* He found himself talked about in Isaiah 61 and he used this to kick start his ministry. *We can discover ourselves by meditating on the word of God and paying attention to the leading of the Holy Spirit.*

4. *Listen to people around you and what they say you can do.* But be careful as you listen. Remember that there are also people whom the enemy will use to discourage you including some of the people close to you. So weigh what people tell you. What they say may not be final.

For example, when I produced the first Gospel Music Album I started by distributing over two hundred of them free of charge. The response was mixed. One day one brother told me that he was from listening to my music and concluded that my voice was too bad to sing. Now because I had been convinced I needed to sing on condition that if people did not like the songs I will like them myself, I told him I will not stop. As I have already pointed out above, *I got this insight from God who Himself liked what He made without looking for other people's commendation in order for Him to proceed.* Every day that He made something in the six days God looked at what He made each day and said it was good in His eyes. *Remember that if David paid attention to his brothers who discouraged him and saw no ability in him killing Goliath, he would not have made history.* He heard them speak but ignored them and went ahead to kill Goliath. Later the same brothers could have participated in chasing the Philistines after David managed to kill Goliath (1 Samuel 17:51-53). For this brother, I continued singing using the same voice up to when he was on sick bed and sung at his funeral and on the day of his burial to the glory of God.

On the same day when the brother close to me discouraged me, I got a text message from another brother close to me who got my music and told me that his family was enjoying my music and that I should not stop. I texted him back and told him that somebody just told me that my voice was bad and wanted me to stop singing. He responded and told me that people get things differently. He told me to *remember the parable of the sower whose seeds fell on different types of soil.* He told me that *the sower depended on the seed that fell on good soil.* This encouraged me to go ahead with the many other responses I have got from my fans.

With this experience, I have come to learn that *I need to look for my fans-my niche out there. I have seen many people being blessed with my songs.* I got encouraged when I saw that on Youtube, they record the number of people who viewed a song or a message. Out of the total they indicate the number of people who like the song and those who do not like the song. These records do not make the producers stop. They only learn from the comments in order to improve.

5. **Look inside yourself.** Carl Jung said, "Your vision will become clear only when you look into your heart. Who looks outside dreams; who looks inside awakens". *Do you want to awaken the sleeping giant in you that God already put in you? Look inside yourself. You will awaken when you look inside yourself. I have awakened to start composing and singing Gospel Songs as a result of looking inside myself.* The writing of this book and many other things I am doing now and are yet to do are a result of my awakening. *I looked inside myself and said there was a lot in me to offload to my generation.* This will make me die a fulfilled life like David who after serving his generation according to God's purpose died. Many other men of God died after serving God's purpose. Jesus Christ, the Apostle Paul, the Apostle Peter and Dr. Myles Munroe are among the many people who add onto my list of those who released what was in them. Some of them on my list are Priscilla and Aquila in the Book of Acts18, Dorcas in Acts9, Queen Esther in the Book of Esther, Ruth and Boaz in the Book of Ruth.

One day while attending a workshop on project appraisal, I took one young lady through what we have done as a family in doing things we have never done before in our lives. I told her how my daughter became a Gospel Artist, how my nephew became a Music Producer and Gospel Artist, how another nephew of mine became a camera man. I also told her how I turned myself into a self-made Gospel Artist. She then exclaimed, "So *you can turn yourself to become anything?"* I answered, "Yes *you can if only you work on your mind."*

6. As Carl Jung put, you also look can look outside yourself and dream about what you are capable of doing and see the gap you are capable feeling in the market by providing a product or service. *After looking inside myself and looking outside me, I have dreams to reach out to the whole world with my products and my services. To help me be energized, I composed the song entitled: "Enlarge my territory O Lord that I may be what you made me to be, to be what you called me to be." This is my dream song.* I dream to reach out to the whole of Africa, to the Americas, to Europe, to Asia and the Islands with my distributed fruit. *I am dreaming going global by launching out my products and services from where I am.* This book and my songs are some of the products designed and produced for the world market. You also are capable of doing the same if you have not started or you have already started in a small way requiring to expand and increase your territory.

7. Look backwards and recall what you used to do as a child -history. I recalled recently that I used to sing a lot when I was young and I also learned that my grandfather Kayekesi used to be a singer. My father also liked singing. I recall that my grandmother on my mother side was a singer. My mother also used to sing. *This gave me evidence that I can sing. All I needed was to pay much more attention to it and invest a lot of time in singing especially to deal with my voice.* This I have been doing ever since as regards singing.

Now, as already stated above, at the time of this writing, I have produced my first gospel album. It may not be in its best state but I have done it. What a source of inspiration for greater things that I am able to do in future! Again as stated above, the Bible in 2 Corinthians13:11encourages us to aim for perfection not to start with perfection. *I have come to learn that many who want to start with perfection may die without producing a product or a service. I have come to learn that versions and editions are an acceptance of the fact that products and services are always being improved.* I went to a Toyota Museum in Nagoya Tokyo where I saw how the Toyota Company developed from a spinning industry to automobiles. We were made to see the first type of Toyota car and after that we were taken to Toyota City. What I saw there were improvements over the years on the Toyota Brand. These were powerful insights on my mind regarding manufacturing and bringing out products and services to the market over years.

The many manufacturers of various goods and services do not give up when they make mistakes. They learn from their mistakes and improve their products. All they do sometimes is to withdraw some of the products from circulation and apologize to the customers. They promise customers to do better with the next products and services. This is not to encourage mediocrity but simply to say that in producing products and services there is room for errors which we should aim to improve on. *Our aim should be perfection. Our aim should be quality. We should aim for good finishing like God did with His creation and making.*

Learn from other people's lives and the efforts of those people who have succeeded in the area you desire to pursue. I have learned a lot from the Men of God like Myles Munroe, Sam Adeyemi, Mensah Otabil, T.D.Jakes, David Abioyemie, David Oyedepo, and Mathew Ashimolowo. By listening to these men of God and others, I have been able to compare some of the teachings I developed before listening to them and validated my work. I have also listened to people like Les Brown, Terri Savelle Foy, Bob Proctor and the late Jim Rohn, Tony Robbins, and Marcus Buckingham who have even motivated me more. *All these have taught me that each one of us has the potential for success like them in our respective areas of strength. Their faith, their attitude to the potential they have, their unique styles of doing things and many more have made me realize I have something unique which my generation is looking for.*

DEFINING YOURSELF AS AN EMPLOYER

You can define yourself in life. Do not let others define you. You need to define yourself. You need to distinguish yourself like Joshua and Caleb in the Bible did (Numbers 14). They distinguished themselves from the majority who doubted by being the few who by faith believed and made a difference in their lives. *Distinguish yourself from the majority who are in doubt and wish to continue as employees and transform yourself into an employer.* Take a step of faith like Abraham who by faith went to a place he did not know (Hebrews11:8-9). Be like Moses who believed God and forsook Egypt because He saw Him who is invisible (Hebrews11:27). *Like Moses you have to depend on seeing the invisible God as you venture into your business wilderness* (Hebrews11:27). *This is business wilderness where at the beginning you may not see the very best in the short term until you conquer business obstacles and find yourself in Canaan land of your business. As you reposition yourself to become an employer, like father Abraham, you may need to depend on the promises and your vision without necessarily knowing where you are heading to.*

There is a place where I used to pack my car when going to one young man's shop. What I noticed was that every time I passed by I found same type of music playing. Every time it was the same type of music. I then got interested in the uniqueness that I had observed. I then asked the brother whose shop was near that shop as to why the man played the same type of music. The brother told me that the man had gone traditional. Before I asked him about the uniqueness of the man's music, the brother was telling me that politicians have made us what we are. I told him that they should not but instead we needed to define ourselves. The politicians are not supposed to define us even though their behavior may affect us is some ways.

The lesson I got from the discussion and the response the brother gave me regarding the man's music is that *we need to define ourselves by being clear about what who we are and what we want to become going forward.* When we do this it protects us from being tossed to and from by people's opinions about us. *Defining ourselves will help us to be focused on our dreams knowing the potential in us and the God who is with us, in us and for us will give us success like He gave success to David.* David believed he was capable of killing of Goliath despite his brothers' and other people's opinions about him.

AWAKENING THE GIANT IN YOU

These insights are basically about you and me repositioning ourselves by realizing what is already in us and deciding to exploit it. It has been designed, as earlier said, in order to provoke you just like I have been provoked in order to have that employer giant in you awakened. The teaching is about you awakening that giant in you who has been laying idle. As Carl Jung put, whom we have referred to already, by looking outside you will dream and by looking inside you will awaken. *It is my desire and hope that you will dream or see visions about yourself and awaken that giant employer in you.*

RELEASING THE EMPLOYER OUT OF YOU

Having repositioned yourself to be an employer in your mind, the next step is for you to become one. As I have been sharing on the importance of repositioning the mind for you to join the few who are employers, a question still remains: *how do you become an employer?* I realize that you and I need to start by hating being employees. *When you hate something, you reach a stage where you don't desire being near it.* This, in my opinion, is the starting point for becoming an employer. Like for me I have already reached this stage. I now hate being an employee to such an extent that I am now dreaming being an employer everyday. I have "fallen in love" with being an employer.

Remember we are told in Songs of Songs 8:7-8 that love is as strong as death and that many waters cannot quench love. Even if you gave all you had for love it would be utterly scorned (despised). In the same way, *if you 'fall in love with' being an employer, you may never love being an employee again*. You will start looking for an exit strategy from your employment. *Those outside come up with a strategy for avoiding becoming employees because of their 'love' for actualizing being employers.* For me having reached this stage, *I am now working towards becoming an employer. I started by questioning what I have been doing all these years.* You also need to come to a point where you realize that being an employee is not the best for you, good as it looks to be.

Remember this is the category in which the majority are. That is why they get less than what they put in because they are too many to share a 'limited piece of cake' called a wage or salary. *When you come to the realization to a point where you look at yourself as a "culprit" of dependence on an employer and then "repent", you will change the course of your direction* like Jacob did while in Uncle Laban's Enterprise.

DECIDING TO BRING OUT THE EMPLOYER IN YOU

You can decide to bring out the employer in you like Jacob did. Abraham and Isaac decided on the onset to be employers. Though it scripture does not explicitly say so, the record shows that they never worked for anybody. People worked for them instead. That is why they were so wealthy that the non-believers envied them. *The patriarchs had wealth and at the same time they were men and women of faith.*

TAKING AN ACTION TO ACTUALIZE YOUR BEING AN EMPLOYER

Deciding to be an employer is not enough but being an employer and an effective employer is what is ultimately needed. Having capacity to employ what you have and make money for yourself is what is key. You don't just decide to bring out the employer in you but have to make sure that you utilize the resources you have effectively to the extent that there are returns on your investment. Jacob took practical steps and changed his situation. It was not too late for him. It is not too late for you and me. *We need to act. This was the secret for the success of the patriarchs-acting when they got the revelation.*

AN EMPLOYER TO BE BORN OUT OF YOU OR THE EMPLOYER TO GROW IN YOU IF YOU ARE ALREADY AN EMPLOYER

All this writing I am doing is to provoke you unto love and good works just as I have been provoked. *There is an employer in you. Let the employer emerge out of your mind given those dreams and ideas you have been having.* Some potential employees are waiting for you to employ them. *Those of you who are already employers, I urge you to continue ploughing and grow your enterprise since you are already holding the plough in your hand.* Don't look behind. We have to say as we go forward in becoming employers, "*There exists an employer in me- I have to release him or her*".

RELEASING WHAT YOU CARRY AS AN EMPLOYER BY BRINGING FORTH WHAT IS IN YOU

The Bible says in Genesis 1:11-12 that God said the earth sprout vegetation plants, yielding seed, and fruit trees bearing fruit. In this fruit was their seed each according to its kind on the earth. The key result of what God said is that it was so. *The earth brought forth vegetation, plants, yielding seed according to their own kinds, and trees beaning fruit in which is their seed, each according to its kind.* God saw that it was good. *He created the earth with the potential to bring forth what was in it.*

From this we can see that when God created the earth one of the products from it was vegetation. The earth brought forth vegetation with seed for continuity being produced from the vegetation. Like the earth, when God created us He put something in us-some potential which we were supposed to bring forth. *We were born pregnant with potential. We were born with seeds of potential waiting to be released to bear fruit.* Each one of us has been carrying a pregnancy which is waiting to be delivered. The pregnancy has been waiting to be brought forth. Myles Munroe in Maximizing your Potential, Munroe (1996), says that the magnitude and depth of human potential on earth has yet to be tapped. Millions are born, live and die, never discovering or exposing the awesome potential that resides within them. He further says that the world needs your potential.

What sustains vegetation on earth is its seed. The vegetation bears fruit carrying a seed which is by nature supposed to be sown and germinates and brings a forest out of it. *God has made you and me in such a way that we are supposed to bear fruit like tree.* In the fruit is seed which is supposed to perpetuate our actions here on earth. For example a possible fruit when you get married is to have a child. A child is in this case fruit of the womb. The child carries a seed with a possibility of having children. This principle applies to any type of fruit that you can bear. The fruit carries with it seed. It could be the fruit of your lips. For example praise is a fruit of the lips. In praise there is seed with potential to produce a fruit by those who hear it. If I sing I am sowing seed into the ears of the hearers. If I keep quiet there will be no fruit in form of a voice coming out from me and as result they will be no seed.

The same principle applies to the word of God. As I share it and it comes out as a fruit of my lips. It is supposed to have a seed to be sown into the hearts of hearers. The voice people hear is the fruit. The seed is in the voice .When you hear my voice as I speak, it plants in you a seed, depending on the type of soil your heart is. The seed is expected to germinate by way of encouragement that you receive and the steps you will take afterwards. The steps you take will also produce a fruit carrying within it a seed for multiplication. That is why we need to make it our aim or our goal to produce from us or bring forth the fruit that will last as Jesus commanded us to. In John 15:16 Jesus commanded us to go and bear fruit that will last. This is what will make you and I more meaningful. When our fruit's seed germinates in people's hearts, they in turn bear fruit. If my fruit has not produced such results, then it may not be the appropriate fruit. Or if nothing is produced from me to affect others in a positive manner, then I am barren according to 2 Peter 1:8. *It is not God's desire for you and me to be ineffective and unfruitful. He created you and me to be effective and fruitful and bear fruit that will last* (John15:16).

In the same way, employers carry within themselves seed to produce a fruit called an enterprise. This enterprise has products or services that are taken to the market. *The fruit which employees produce is their labour to the extent that they add value to the employer's fruit.* It is this that makes a difference between the two. The type of seed sown determines what is reaped according to Galatians6:7. When the products are sown in the market, the owner of the enterprise gets the fruit of the harvest from his/her enterprise when profits are made like a hard working farmer who is patient to get the harvest from his/her crop (2Timothy2:6).

CHAPTER 9: THE EMPLOYER IN YOU AND THE DOMINION BUSINESS CYCLE

I take it that you have at this point realized that there is an employer in you and have repositioned yourself from having an employee mind to having an employer mind. Further, you have decided to release the employer in you by taking an affirmative action like Jacob did. You have taken the initial steps in realizing the employer in you. *Now you need to go through what I have called the Dominion Business Cycle for you to fully realize the employer in you by ultimately having dominion over the earth and the resources in it.*

GOD'S ORIGINAL INTENT FOR YOU AND ME

When God blessed man and told him to be fruitful, to multiply, to fill the earth and subdue and ultimately dominate, who was to own this process? Are you and I able to see the ownership principle in this? When God created the earth and gave it to Adam and Eve, they chose to be tenants when they should have been landlords. *I would rather be a landlord rather than be a tenant, a boss rather than being a subordinate, an employer rather than be an employee. It is better being an employer. I would rather I became an employer than being an employee. I don't know for you.*

What you see in Genesis 1:28 when God introduced the dominion mandate to man is that *He commissioned man to be a business person. He actually told man to do business by going through the dominion business cycle* as illustrated below in the Investment Arena as the process required for one to transition from having an employee mind to having an employer mind and being an employer in reality.

UNDERSTANDING GOD'S ORIGINAL INTENTION FOR YOU TO HAVE DOMINION OVER HIS CREATION

As we have already established, Man was created to have dominion here on earth. This was to become a reality by man undertaking business. Knowing this truth sets you free. Genesis1:26-28 and Psalms8 tells you and me why God created us. *We are designed to dominate by doing business. This is the DNA in us-to do business and dominate.* This domination mandate can be seen in Psalms8. The Psalmist points out that God has made the son of man a little lower than angels and has crowned him with glory and honour. Even when this is a prophetic utterance about Jesus Christ as portrayed in Hebrwes2:5-9, we are included in the equation. God has crowned us with glory and honour. In doing this He has made all he created to be subject to us.

In making this dominion a reality, we are supposed to put into practice what the late man of God Myles Munroe called the four business laws. These according to him are: being fruitful, multiplying the fruit, distributing the fruit and subduing the earth with that fruit. This ultimately leads to domination. When we go through this process we are establishing the fact that we were created for dominion.

WHO WE ARE IN GOD'S SIGHT

In Galatians 6:16, we are told that we are the Israel of Christ. Ephesians2:12 tells us that at one time we were alienated from the commonwealth of Israel and from the covenants. Now in Christ, we have been brought into peace with God-we are no longer alienated. We are sons of the Most High God the creator and owner of the heavens and the earth (Psalms24:1). *We have a rich Father and we are rich as a result!*

GOD HAS ALREADY GIVEN US ALL WE NEED WHATEVER THE EXCUSE

As far as 2Peter1:3-4 is concerned, God's divine nature has given us all we need for life and godliness. *What we need for life and godliness is not poverty but wealth in all areas of our lives*. Those elements that make us enjoy life of faith are ours. For example 1Timothy6:17 says that *God richly, not poorly, provides us with everything to enjoy*. None of us enjoys poverty. Someone has said that poverty is a consequence of deprivation not an intention.

THE DOMINION CYCLE-THE BUSINESS CYCLE

Remember that you and I carry a blessing for dominion. This dominion cycle was confirmed by God concerning the descendants of Abraham in Genesis22.This is further confirmed in Galatians3:13-14. We are to share in the blessing of Abraham who was not only a man of faith but also a man of wealth according to Genesis24:1, 35. *For dominion to take place, you need to go through what I have called the dominion cycle.* We can refer to the dominion cycle as the business cycle. The late man of God Myles Munroe called the dominion elements as the business laws. The dominion cycle is that for you to dominate you need to:

- Be fruitful
- Multiply the fruit
- Market your fruit

- Subdue the market with your fruit

- Then dominate with your influence through your fruit.

- *You serve your generation with what you were born to serve them* (Acts 13:36).

The dominion cycle is there as a process for you to dominate. For it to be a reality you need to go through the cycle in the order God presented it to Adam and Eve when He created them.

SUBDUE

BE FRUITFUL

FILL THE
EARTH

(MARKET
YOUR FRUIT)

MULTIPLY

FIGURE 5: THE DOMINION BUSINESS CYCLE

GOD GAVE MAN SEED TO START WITH AND TOLD HIM WHAT TO DO WITH THE SEED

God told man to behold what He had given him- plants with seed in them (Genesis1:29). Further, God told man to manage what he had given him (Genesis2:15).As already pointed out, **God gave man business to do on the onset.** Each one of us has some business to do whether we are doing it or not. **God put man in a position of an employer.** Again as pointed out above, we see it from Adam to Noah. We also see it in Abraham and Isaac. These were employers. Of course they employed servants who were in a sense employees.

DOMINION IS AN INSIDE MATTER

Inside each one of us is the capacity to dominate. We each have the earth as our domination arena. What is true for each one of us is that there are areas of domination in the earth for you and I to dominate. Imagine that you were Adam or Eve and God gives you the terms of reference in Genesis Chapter 1 and 2! Psalms24:1 says that the earth is God's and all its fullness. Now in Psalms115:16 says that God has given the earth to sons of men. This means that you are the earth's shareholder. There is a part of the earth for your domination. Remember, God's main objective for creating the earth was you. And Psalms8:5-6 says that God is mindful about you and that He has given you dominion over all His creation. *You have the dominion gene within you requiring to be actualized. A Mr. Les Brown puts it you have something you brought to the universe.*

IMAGINE YOU WERE ADAM OR EVE IN THE GARDEN OF EDEN!

Imagine you were in the Garden of Eden and God blessed you and commanded you to be fruitful, to multiply, to fill the earth and to subdue so that ultimately you dominate! What would have rang in your mind? Meanwhile He is telling you all that at a time He does not give you cash - is capital! Where would you have started from? To look for a job to raise capital while you are in the Garden of Eden? Meanwhile God is telling you behold the trees and the seed in them and that they shall be food for you! Meanwhile this God says tend the garden. On top of this He even gives you a spouse even without you settling!

THE NEED FOR DOMINION REPOSITIONING AS AN EMPLOYER

You need to reposition yourself into the dominion mandate position in which God put you when He created you. A number of people are in a wrong position or wrong place and doing the wrong thing. *There is an appropriate position designed for you by God in which He wants you to be located. This will require repositioning yourself in your mind from having an employee mind to having and employer mind.* After repositioning, you will need to take strategic actions like Jacob did to actualize your ideas. God will then direct your steps as you plan your way and commit your plans to Him.

God speaks to you *to open your eyes so that you could see, arise and walk through the land to move yourself to a right position* (Genesis13:14-18). You could have been ignoring His voice. Deutoromy8:7-8 points out that the LORD our God desires to bring us into a good land. He wants to bring us to a land with streams and pools of water, a land with springs flowing in the valleys and hills. He desires that we possess the land and dominate the resources in that land for our prosperity. God in Joshua6:1-2, told Joshua to see that He had given him Jericho for his possession. You need to have the capacity to see and reposition yourself as an employer.

CHAPTER 10: ON A JOURNEY TO DOMIMION AS AN EMPLOYER
(AN ENTREPRENUER)

Your journey, including mine, to dominion was started when God created man and blessed him and conferred on him the capacity to undertake business by being fruitful, multiply, fill the earth, subdue it and ultimately dominate the earth as illustrated below:

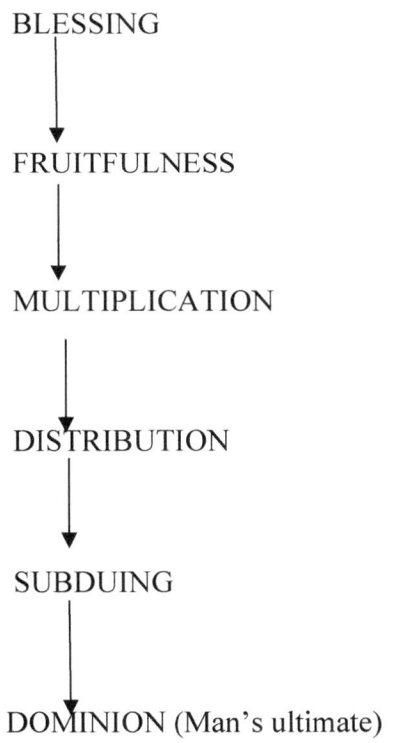

BLESSING

↓

FRUITFULNESS

↓

MULTIPLICATION

↓

DISTRIBUTION

↓

SUBDUING

↓

DOMINION (Man's ultimate)

FIGURE 6: THE DOMINION MANDATE FROM GOD

As already indicated above, I have called the above illustration as the dominion life cycle or dominion business cycle.

THE DOMINION BUSINESS CYCLE FOR YOU AS AN EMPLOYER

Remember in the beginning as we are told in Genesis 1:28, God created man and blessed him to dominate the earth by undertaking business on earth by:

- Being fruitful
- multiplying his fruit,
- filling the earth with his fruitfulness (The Late man of God Myles Munroe called it distribution) and
- Subduing using his fruitfulness and management of the multiplied fruit.
- Dominating the earth which is the ultimate for man.

As an employer, when you dominate that area of business in which you go through the dominion cycle it will give you the results you desire to achieve business wise.

TALAZHEYI- MIND YOUR OWN BUSINESS (DOING YOUR OWN WORK QUIETLY TO EARN YOUR OWN LIVING AS AN EMPLOYER)

In Lunda Language, my mother tongue, they have a word called "Talazheyi" to mean mind your business. In Lunda language, ***TALAZHEYI*** means ***mind your own business***. To mind your own business means that each one of us has some business to do which we are to mind and work with our own hands. ***The question is whose business is it that I mind for now?*** Is this my business or someone else's business? Who is in control of the business? Who has the final say and who gets the biggest share of the business? To mind your business means that you pay attention to the work of your hands and work with your own hands. For example what I am doing now by writing this Book is minding my business. I have my specialization to bring me results.

This principle is used in 1Thessalonians4:11 which talks about **minding your own business. That is paying attention to your own work and not to mind someone else's work. Your own work is key.** You having ownership of your work to quietly earn your own living. ***The source of your living in terms of resources is designed to come from you doing your own work. Your livelihood is designed come from you undertaking your own business.*** You also consider what we are told in 2Thessalonians3:12-13. We are told that with quietness we work and eat our own bread. This is referred to as well doing. We are told that we should not grow weary in doing good. This doing good is undertaking our own work to earn us a living. We can then say that ***business is connected to doing something good.*** This is what we have been encouraged to do as believers. We are discouraged from any form of idleness.

AN EMPLOYER AS A BUSINESS PERSON

An employer is a business person. Who is a business person? In my opinion a business person, as opposed to being a busy body, is a person who gets involved in resolving challenges in the affairs of others because they have been looking for him or her for a solution. He finds himself among customers or his products or service reach customers because his product or service is needed by those customers. He/she is fulfilling the working definition we have established below regarding business.

FOUR THINGS A MAN SHOULD DO ACCORDING TO THE JEWS

According to John Gills Salem Web Network Commentary, the Jews say, "There are four things a man should constantly attend with all his might and they are these: the law, good works, prayer and 'the way of the earth' or 'Business'; if a tradesman to his trade, if a merchant to his merchandise, if man of war to war."

DEFINITIONS OF BUSINESS

Lewis Henry defines business as, "Human activity directed towards producing and acquiring wealth through buying and selling of goods. The term business means continuous production and distribution of goods and services with the aim of earning profits under certain market conditions.

According to Ecclastiastes9:10, business can be defined to be whatsoever your hand finds to do, where you invest your energy to work, undertake planning for it and applying wisdom and knowledge to it to give you results.

THE KAYEKESI WORKING DEFINITION OF BUSINESS

We are going to use a very long definition of business that I have crafted using my understanding of Genesis1:28, Genesis9:1, 7, Deuteronomy8:18 and other scriptures including business literature for the purpose of this teaching on business.

Business from the Biblical perspective is about *being blessed* and as a result *bringing forth fruit*; the fruit *being multiplied*; what has been multiplied *being distributed* to customers/clients; who in turn *perceive* our product/service to be a *unique* and *superior brand* and *decide to consume more of our brand* resulting in *increased demand for our product/ service* and as such *we gain customer loyalty*; resulting in the *creation of a niche* that makes a decision to continuously demand our product/service; *our customers* in turn *share their experience* about our product/service's *superiority* with other customers or we ourselves do so through *marketing strategies* like advertising; resulting in *increased market share*; that results in *increased sales;* leading to *profitability*; resulting in *increased shareholder returns*; resulting in *increased, acquired* and *established wealth;* ending up with *subduing in that area of specialization*; the *ultimate being domination.*

BUSINESS FACILITATES WEALTH CREATION FOR AN EMPLOYER

Apart from ill-gotten wealth and inherited wealth from parents and other sources of wealth (Proverbs 19:14), *business facilitates the acquisition of wealth.* However, it is not everybody who undertakes business who ends up being wealth. Remember Ecclesiates 10:15 telling us that a fool's work wearies him for he does not know the way to the city. *Working or engaging in business in itself is not a guarantee for wealth acquisition, but it is a prerequisite for wealth creation.* There are also other factors that can help one create and build wealth which drives a business undertaking which may not be discussed here.

AN EMPLOYER AS AN ENTREPRENEUR WHO IS A BUSINESS UNDERTAKER

An employer is an entrepreneur who is a business undertaker. He or she is a business undertaker who innovates and creates solutions that are products or services to be sold to the market to get profit and ultimately create wealth.

ENTREPRENEURSHIP AS ONE OF THE DETERMINANTS OF WEALTH CREATION

According to Drucker, entrepreneurship is an act of innovation that involves endowing existing resources with new wealth producing capacity. Stevenson says entrepreneurship is a process by which individuals pursue and exploit opportunities irrespective of the resources they control.

AN ENTREPRENEUR ACCORDING TO DR. MYLES MUNROE

According to the late man of God Myles Munroe, as I listened to him on Youtube, an entrepreneur has discovered an idea that would not leave him or her. When he or she decides to produce a product or service from that idea, it means his or her business has began.

A JOB IS FOR AN EMPLOYEE WHILE BUSINESS (WORK) IS FOR AN EMPLOYER (ENTREPRENEUR)

Bear in mind that we have used the word employer as a synonym to entrepreneur. So *saying that there is an employer in you is the same as saying that there is an entrepreneur in you. It is the entrepreneur who has ventured into a business undertaking and has ended up having employees to work for him or her.*

Drawing lessons from the Man of God Myles Munroe regarding a job and work, he points out that a job is what you are paid to do while work is what you were born to do. According to him, *a genuine business person seeks to manifest an idea, a dream, and a seed that is trapped in them. The reproduction of the idea, to him, is the beginning of your business.* He further says that each one of us has a gift hidden inside and that gift in us turns out to be our business. No wonder the Bible in Proverbs18:16 says a man's gift, not his education, makes room for him and ushers him into the presence of great men. While an employee can be fired, a business person cannot because he or she is a carrier of a gift that is inside him or her. Business is equivalent to one's work which is embedded in him or her. *It is your work or your business which can make you rich not your job.* So the business person becomes an owner of the means of production by paying the employee for him or her to offer him the desired labour. This ownership makes him or her become a shareholder who benefits from dividends instead getting a wage or a salary which is the reward of an employee.

EMPLOYERS OR ENTREPRENUERS AS FRUIT PRODUCERS: YOU SHALL KNOW THEM BY THEIR FRUIT

The Bible says that you shall know people by their fruit which they produce. *If we shall be known by our fruit, then it means we have the potential to produce fruit with the seed in us.* In Genesis 1:11 God spoke to the earth to produce plants yielding seed. The fruit from the trees was designed to contain seed inside it. The seed is what assures the multiplication in trees.

THE STARTING POINT FOR WEALTH CREATION

As already pointed out, thinking for yourself hundred percent is the starting point for wealth creation for yourself instead of creating wealth for an employer. *You spend your hundred percent time to create your own wealth. It is wealth creation which results from allocating hundred percent of your work thought which leads to wealth acquisition making you a wealth person.* Though Jacob was still working for Laban, he had in a way moved from thinking for Laban but was thinking about Himself as a partner in the business. Remember that there relations had changed from employee-employer relations to employer- employee relations as business partners. Jacob had transformed himself to what are being called corporate entrepreneurs today.

UNDERTAKING WEALTH ACQUISITION AND WEALTH DISTRIBUTION LIKE FATHER ABRAHAM, FATHER ISAAC AND FATHER JACOB WHO WERE EMPLOYERS

So far we have discussed the importance of repositioning yourself from having an employee mind to having an employer mind so the reality that Abraham, Isaac and Jacob experienced can be your reality as well. This will really make you see the completeness of the reality of you being redeemed by Christ so that you can share in the blessing of Abraham as written in Galatians3:13-14. Father Abraham was a man of faith, a friend of God and a rich man materially as indicated in Romans4:17 James2:23 and Genesis 24:35. *The blessing of Abraham, of which Isaac and Jacob were partakers, are yours and mine to partake since we are now the Israel of Christ according to Galatians6:16.* Ephesians2:11-12 says that you who were strangers to the covenants and commonwealth of Israel have now become partakers of the commonwealth of Israel. As you reposition yourself and release the employer in you and see to it that you apply business wisdom, understanding and knowledge, you can see yourself acquiring wealth and use it for the purpose of the kingdom. This will confirm what 1 Timothy6:17-19 talks about commanding those who are rich not to put themselves high but to humble themselves and *use their riches to:*

- *do good works*
- *to share*
- *to be generous ,*

in this present age. By so doing, we are told they will establish an eternal foundation and store for themselves treasure which is truly treasure in heaven. I trust this is talking about you as you actualize dominion in your life as an employer. When you become rich in material things here on earth, you will then be commanded by the leadership to do good works, to share and to be generous. *God bless you for repositioning yourself to be what He made you to be and to be what He called you to be-an employer.* HALLELUYAH

MOVING BEYOND WEALTH CREATION TO WEALTH ACCUMULATION OR ACQUISITION

Wealth creation does not necessary imply wealth accumulation for yourself. *A faithful employee like Jacob might create wealth but the wealth ends up being accumulated by Laban who is an owner*. It is not until you realize the secret of wealth acquisition shall you be vigilant to know whether the wealth you are creating is yours or for the employer. Are you simply creating wealth for your employer or you are accumulating wealth for yourself as an employer?

MOVING OUT OF YOUR WILDERNESS

Moses who in the wilderness for 40 years as a shepherd. He went to Mount Sinai for 40 days and 40 nights as he received the Ten Commandments. Jesus was in the wilderness for 40 days and 40 nights and the Apostle Paul went into Arabia before he ventured into ministry. David was in the bush tending his father's sheep before he became king and Joseph was in Prison before he became a ruler in Egypt. *Like these and many others who have gone before us, we also may be in some wilderness in the course of our lives and career go. This wilderness may be business wilderness. However, there is a time, when, after picking all the lessons God had for us to learn and acquire, we are supposed to get out of our wilderness and move forward towards our destiny.* For me that time to get out of my wilderness is now.

MOVING OUT OF BUSINESS WILDERNESS AND FOCUSING TOWARDS DOMINATING IN AN AREA OF BUSINESS ON EARTH

Just like in ordinary life where we may find ourselves wandering in the wilderness going round circles, the same may apply to business if not focussed. If not focussed, we may find ourselves into business wilderness wondering like the Israelites wondered for forty years in the wilderness. That is why business may prove not to be an easy road and that is why a good number of people would rather become employees. *The cream of this world are the employers who have chosen to differentiate themselves from the majority.* Before reaching the break- even point in your business, you may be required to go through moments of learning and acquiring ideas to give us direction. Thank God that Jesus who is the way, the truth and the life is able to give us the way even when there seems to be no way (John14:6).

The secret in a business undertaking is to keep on learning and applying what we learn to our day to day business encounters. Remember that there is always a breakeven point for a given business if we are doing things right. People around us can then see that we were serious and meant business as we took various decisions when they see us impacting our world with our distributed fruit

MOVING FORWARD IN BUSINESS TO ACTUALIZE YOUR GOD GIVEN DOMINION

Business is designed to grow. *Being static at one point is not the mind of God.* God's mind for us is to go forward towards achieving our business plans. Proverbs16:3 says that commit your plans to the LORD and he will make them succeed. I believe this includes committing our **business plans to Him.** When we come up with business plans, we have to commit them to the Almighty God to ensure their success. God then becomes a partner with us in our implementation. Psams37:23 says that God orders the steps of a good and He delights in his way. Your way is designed in the plans you commit to Him and then *He orders your steps as you implement the plans you commit to Him.* So God delights in your plans.

THE PROCESS REQUIRED ON THE DOMINION JOURNEY FOR ONE TO TRANSITION FROM HAVING AN EMPLOYEE MIND TO HAVING AN EMPLOYER MIND.

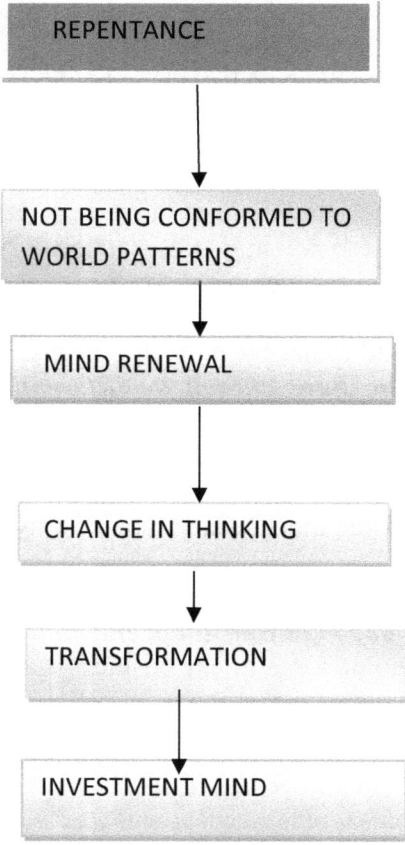

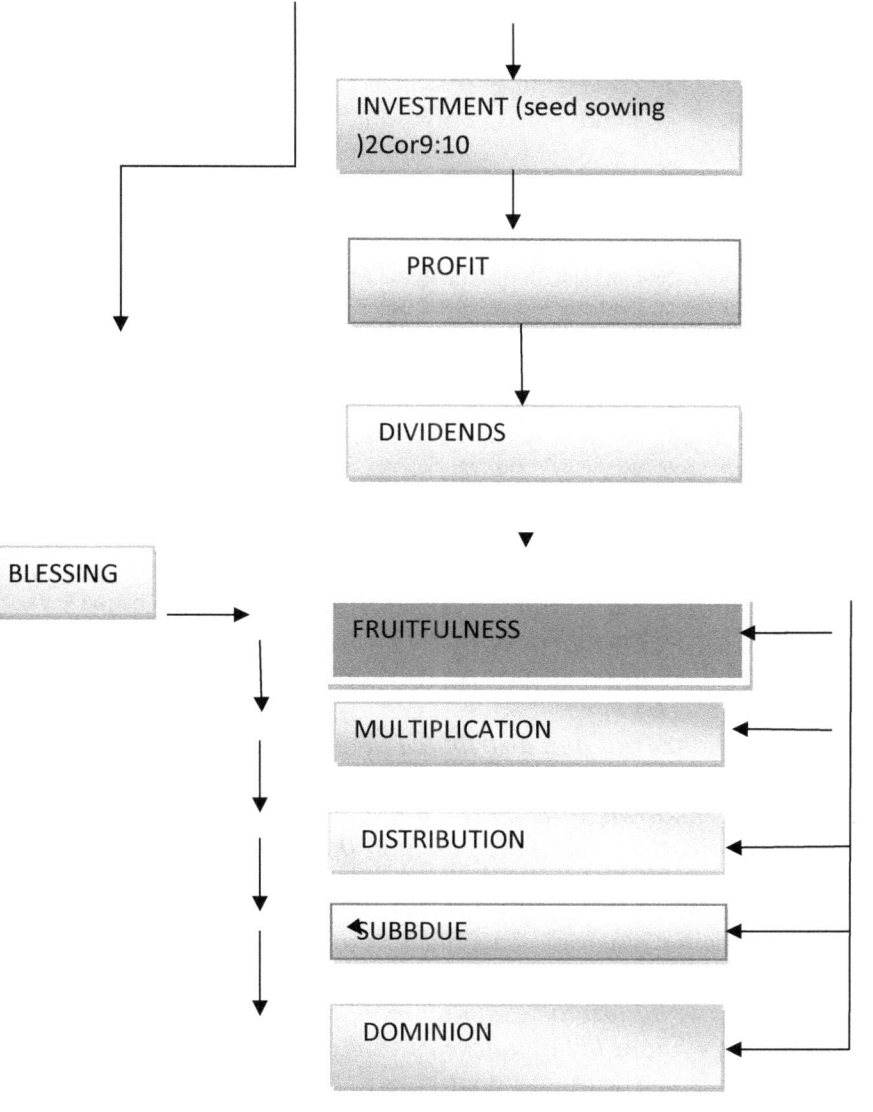

FIGURE 4: PROCESS FOR TRANSITIONING FROM EMPLOYEE TO EMPLOYER

The above illustration gives the process required for one to transition from having an employee mind to having an employer mind. *An employer has an investment mind which makes a difference between him or her and an employee.*

In order to make a difference, the following questions have to be answered:

- What is God's plan/mind for me?

- What are the good thoughts or plans God has for me?

- What changes should take place in my mind?

- Where am I now?

- Where should I be from now onwards?

- What should I do to be where I should be?

In order for you to transform yourself to a level where you have to have an investment mind so that you share in dividends, you need to realize the key aspects to getting dividends. *An investment mind requires that you go through the process of fruitfulness, multiplication and then distribution.* You have the capacity to multiply (Genesis1:28, Genesis9:2, 7). After multiplying, you need to distribute your multiplied fruit. *Distribution is about going global.* The command from Jesus was that you and I have to go and bear fruit and fruit that will last (John15:16, Matthew28:19). So *you need not only to multiply your fruit but you also need to distribute it so that the process is completed leading to subduing and domination. When you have been fruitful then undertaken multiplication of your fruit and distributed the multiplied fruit, subduing and dominion take place automatically. Where you and I have failed and where we need breakthrough is more on multiplication and distribution of that which we create by using the potential that God has put in us*.

On fruitfulness, many have tried to produce some fruit but their failure is on the fruit not being much or stopping to produce the fruit altogether. Others have produced much fruit which has not been marketed. *They are like a mango tree which produces many mangoes and when they ripen, they drop and rot without being marketed and consumed.* If we can bear much fruit, multiply the fruit and distribute it, we may even go to sleep provided we have put in place a mechanism for monitoring the distributed fruit. This is at the subduing level at which you see to it that the needs of the customers are met through customer satisfaction. *If the subduing aspect is managed by getting feedback from customers to improve the quality of our products and services, then domination in that area of business is assured.* This becomes our winning formula to becoming what God created us for- that is to have dominion here on earth!

CHAPTER 11: THE 3 INGREDIENTS FOR BUILDING, ESTABLISHING AND FILLING (POPULATING) YOUR BUSINESS HOUSE

To build a business house you need wisdom, to establish the business you need understanding and to populate it you need knowledge as pointed out in Proverbs 24:3-4. Provides 9:1 says that wisdom has built her house. ***Wisdom is a business house builder.*** This means that as an employer, you can build your business house using wisdom. To establish the business house, you need understanding. And to fill the business house with precious treasures that customers out there will be willing to pay for to acquire the treasures from us, knowledge is the material to use. We can then see that *wisdom, understanding and knowledge are key business building, business establishing and business populating materials that can make a business successful.*

GET WISDOM, GET UNDERSTANDING (INSIGHT) FOR YOU TO BUILD AND ESTABLISH YOUR BUSINESS HOUSE AS AN EMPLOYER

No wonder we are told in Proverbs4:7 that in all our getting, we have to get wisdom and have to get understanding (insight). Without understanding, this discussion will not have any meaning to you. This because your understanding could be fixed to the extent that in fact not everybody cannot be an employer. Of course that is true but *understanding will make you realize you could be among those who are not supposed to be employees*. Remember that you are where you find yourself as matter of choice. As we have stated above, it is said in my mother tongue that **a better tail is one that you grow on your own instead of a borrowed one**. *This refers to independence, self-reliance and ownership.* It means that *when you are the owner you can decide what, when and how to use your own* without conditionality that arise from being dependent on another person's thing.

You will understand that ownership is better than when your life depends on the employer's goodwill. It is like when you realize that although the majority are tenants, you abhor or hate yourself being a tenant. You can then start working towards being a landlord. Depending on your understanding, you may choose forever to be a tenant and you may never own your own house. Thank God for most people in villages. They understand this principle such that most of them build their own houses, simple ones as some of them may be. These also engage themselves in doing their own work. So you see an aspect of ownership in them. Wisdom and understanding are key in building a business house and establishing it respectively.

BUSINESS WISDOM NEEDED TO BUILD THE EMPLOYER IN YOU

James1:5 says that if you lack wisdom, ask God. We need wisdom in order to undertake life's endeavors. The more of the stature of Christ we attain, the wiser we become. Christ is our wisdom from God as stated in 1Corinthians1:30. By wisdom God formed the earth as stated in Proverbs3:19. By wisdom He made the heavens as pointed out in Psalms136:5. By wisdom a House is built as stated in Proverbs24:3.This can be a physical house, your body and my body as an earthly tent, the church as the household of God or a business undertaking. The Bible tells us that wisdom is the principle thing. It is more important than having money.

I believe that wisdom can be displayed in different types and used in each of the various areas like the following business areas:

- Farming wisdom
- Construction wisdom
- Singing wisdom
- Communication wisdom
- Hospitality wisdom
- Administrative wisdom
- Marketing wisdom and so forth.

REDEEMING TIME AS A SIGN OF BUSINESS WISDOM FOR YOU AS AN EMPLOYER

The use of time wisely by redeeming it is a sign of wisdom. A foolish person is one who does not understand the will of God as regards getting the best out of every given opportunity. If we want wisdom from above, including business wisdom, let us know God's will and do it. In Ephesians 5:15-17, we are told to be wise by redeeming time and that we make the most of time. In Luke 12:41-43, Jesus talked about a wise manager. To Him *a wise manager is the one who is faithful in utilizing the opportunity given to him to manage the master's resources.* So what a good manager does is to understand the master's will and utilize time appropriately. *The employer as the owner of an enterprise expects time to be utilized wisely to marshal resources into their consumable state for the market.* This is required in a business enterprise for it to increase its productivity and hence profitability

BUSINESS UNDERSTANDING NEEDED IN ESTABLISHING YOURSELF AS AN EMPLOYER

By understanding God established the heavens and as we have indicated above and by understanding we are told that we have to establish a house (Proverbs3:19-20). *Understanding is key because it answers why we should do what we have to do. Your understanding of the basis for doing something makes you venture into it something with conviction and passion. It acts as fuel that keeps moving you like a vehicle or an aeroplane in covering distances despite the terrain.*

As pointed out above, the Bible in Proverbs24:3-4 talks about three key components which can be used in the three aspects of coming up with a house: building, establishing and filling the house (what I call populating the house). For building a house we are told that wisdom is needed. For establishing it understanding is required. Knowledge is required for filling (populating) the house with rare and precious treasures. Applying this to a business undertaking, we can say that by wisdom, business is built up, by understanding it is established. By knowledge a business undertaking has rare and precious treasures. *We have to establish a business well by applying understanding (insight). It is cardinal for you to establish yourself as an employer by using understanding in your business. So understanding is the material that can be used to establish a business for you as an employer. Get understanding and get established.*

BUSINESS KNOWLEDGE NEEDED POPULATE YOUR BUSINESS HOUSE AND MAKE THE RELEASED EMPLOYER IN YOU A REALITY

Remember in Hosea4:6, God said my people are perishing because of lack of knowledge. Since God used knowledge to populate the earth with pleasant treasures (Proverbs3:20) and we are told that by knowledge a house is filled with pleasant treasures, knowledge is key in bringing results in your business house as an employer. *Knowledge will bring to reality ideas into tangible things and will be used in managing what we will have built and established. It is knowledge that will cause the business to have rarity and unique products that will attract customers and create customer loyalty.*

WHEN YOU RELEASE YOUR POTENTIAL AS AN EMPLOYER YOU EARN OR REAP DIVIDENDS OR INTEREST AS A RESULT

Jacob while an employee and later repositioning himself as an employer experienced the law of sowing and reaping as regards being an employee and being an employer. Despite Laban confessing to Jacob that he had brought a turnaround in his company by putting in his best, *Jacob received what sowing labour ends up reaping* (Genesis30:27-30). *Although Jacob worked for Laban with all his strength he reaped what an employee deserves-wages. That is what 1Timothy5:18 says that a laborer is due his wages not his dividends or his interest earned.* When Jacob repositioned himself and took a different position within the same place, his story changed dramatically. *God who sees one's sowing makes one reap what he or she has been sown using His special reward system.*

In the case of Jacob, *God looked forward to a day when he would promote himself to a level where he sowed his seed as an employer.* Immediately Jacob started sowing the seed of an employer, God got involved in the drama that transferred wealth from Laban to Jacob. *I believe God is waiting for His children to reposition themselves so that He can be involved in the wealth creation acquisition drama for His children.* He did it with Jacob and He is able to do it for us if we shall reposition ourselves and take the right positions as employers and release the employers in us. *In the same way He worked with in Jacob's wealth creation and acquisition, God can show us in our dreams what we can do to bring about turnaround in our economic status. If we release ourselves as employers by sowing employer seeds, we expect to reap according to what an employer sows.* The type of sowing and reaping that you get at the end of the day is a reward to you according to what you will have sown. *If you release yourself into the labor market as labor you reap what labor deserves. But when you release yourself as an employer, the law of sowing and reaping comes into play accordingly. You reap dividends or interest if you are the provider of capital as the owner of the business venture.*

WHAT IS LACKING MAY NOT BE A MONEY PROBLEM BUT A LACK OF WISDOM, UNDERSTANDING AND KNOWLEDGE.

For many people, they say the reason for them not becoming employers is lack of capital. I used to think like that some years back but now I have a different understanding. *Though the Bible says that money is the answer, it also mentions wisdom as an answer and points out wisdom as having an advantage of money* (Ecclasiastes7:26). Money has limitations. Further money is simply a measure of value. *What this means is that what you need to have first is not money but value. And value is created using wisdom, understanding and knowledge.* We have above pointed out that the Bible tells us that God by wisdom built the earth; by understanding He established the heavens and by knowledge He made dew fall on earth. The same three components God used in creation and making are the same components we are told to use in building a house, establishing it and filling it with great treasure. This as we have pointed above applies also to building a business house. However, very few people have applied these three components in their business transactions. ***The moment you pay attention to applying the three components to your life and to your business transactions, then you will attract money to yourself and the aspects of your wellbeing.***

Again we have so far established that ***when God put Adam and Eve in the Garden of Eden, he did not give them money but put potential in them and in the resources that he put in the earth***. He told man to be fruitful, to multiply the fruit, use the fruit to fill the earth and then subdue the earth resulting in man actualizing the dominion God gave him. This is the dominion cycle. ***Remember dominion is a given thing that you and I need to actualize***. In order for man to fulfill this dominion cycle, He told him to behold the seed in the trees around him that bore fruit (Genesis1:29). ***In order for man to go through the dominion cycle, he was to have a mix of the potential in him and the potential that was put in the resources.***

This is called exploitation of natural resources to meet the needs for man. All that man needed was to apply wisdom, understanding and knowledge in undertaking business to meet his needs. ***In so doing, man would be able to exchange his value added products or services for money. It is at this point that the money discussion comes in.*** So ***check yourself to see whether the real problem has been a money problem or a lack of wisdom, understanding and knowledge.*** But ***you will realize that for many of us the challenge has been a wisdom, understanding and knowledge constraint.*** When you undertake a constraint analysis of your impediments to becoming an employer, one of the constraints would come out as a lack of wisdom, understanding and knowledge. ***For you to overcome this constraint, you will need to get wisdom, understanding and knowledge from God through prayer and meditation. This is the key to your business success as an employer.***

CHAPTER 12: THE IMPORTANCE OF VALUE IN THE MARKET PLACE PROVIDED BY YOU AS AN EMPLOYER

"The Market Place pays for value" Jim Rohn

According to Jim Rohn, the market place pays for value. He quotes his teacher Mr. Shaw who told him that it is not what you get that makes you valuable, it is what you become. He was told that *we get paid for bringing value to the market and that we do not get paid for time but for value brought to the market place. If you are not valuable to the market place, you do not get much money.* He was further told to set goals that would make something out of him. So he was advised to start the process of change and that *if he was to change everything was to change for him. With this advice, he embarked on setting goals and undertook personal development that transformed his life tremendously.* Even you and I can experience the same if we embark on adding value on ourselves to take to the market.

MONEY IS NOT OUT THERE, IT IS INSIDE YOU AND ME

Money is not out there but is actually inside you and me. Remember that money is the measure of value. *As you add value to yourself and also add value to the resources around you and beyond you, the added value attracts money.* For example, schooling should be intended to add value on you so that you can sell that value in the market place. That is why there is value added tax. *You then sell value for money.* Others sell their value for a price called a wage or a salary while *others are smart enough to sell their value for a dividend or for interest. When you choose to be an employee, the employer buys your value and pays a wage or salary for it. If you choose to become an employer, you sell your value for a dividend or interest.*

THE SECRET BEHIND VALUE IN THE MARKET PLACE

As already pointed out above, Jim Rohn says that what you sell to the market is not your time but your value. He points out that the market buys value. He further points out that in order to have value that will be bought in the market, you need to engage in personal development so that you can be able to produce the required value for the market. *Put value on your products and services by bearing in mind that the customers out there are looking for your value to buy.* That is why money is simply a measure of value. This means that money is used to measure the value of a good or service. What this means is that *if you want to make money in the market place, you need to engage yourself in value addition to your products or services which you then sell for money in the market place.*

FROM INTAGIBLE TO TANGIBLE THINGS

Imagination can lead you into creation of things in your mind which you can translate into tangible things. The Bible in Jeremiah6:19 talks about the fruit of your thoughts. So it means that your mind or your thoughts as you imagine can produce a fruit and that fruit can be made tangible when it is translated into a tangible product or service. *It all starts with your mind. It starts with your imagination.* Of course the type of imagination matters. The type of imagination determines the type of product and services you produce.

SEE VALUE IN YOURSELF AND ASK HOW MANY DOLLARS IT IS PUTTING IN YOUR POCKET

"Try not to become a man of success, but rather try to become a man of value" Albert Einstein.

Have you assessed your current and future value? At what price will you be willing to sell your value? Is your value worth a wage or a dividend? It is important that you see in yourself and ask how many dollars it is putting in your pocket. As Albert Einstein put it, you should not become a man of success, but rather you have to try and become a man or woman of value. This will in turn make you successful. This is complimented as already pointed out about what Jim Rohn said that the market does not pay you for your time but you are paid for the value you take to the market. *It is, however, your value taken to the right market that will make you put more dollars in your pocket than it would do if you took the same value in a wrong market.* You realize that pork which is cherished in some cultures is not cherished in others. This is true for many products and services. *See the value in yourself and ask the type of products or services it can produce and be sold in the right market to give you the dollars you exchange for your value.* Remember, we have already pointed out that money is a measure of value.

SEEING OPPORTUNITIES IN THE MARKET WHILE OTHERS ARE SEEING CHALLENGES

Jack Ma, the founder of Alibaba has said that *you need to worry about what the majority are not worried about; that is opportunity*. You need to see opportunities in the market place while others are worried about challenges. In fact *business is said to be giving solutions to a challenge in order to be paid by those for whom you resolve those challenges. Genesis8:22 points out that every aspect of seasons in the earth provides a market for selling goods and services.* It points out that as long as the earth endures seed time and harvest time, cold and heat, summer and winter, day and night endure for over. What this means is that *there is always a market for anything you think of producing. All you need is to identify those markets, be fruitful, multiply your fruit and distribute it to the identified markets.*

SEEING VALUE IN THE RESOURCES AROUND TO TRANSFORM THEM INTO A PRODUCT OR SERVICE TO BENEFIT YOU AS AN EMPLOYER

For you to be fruitful as you move through the dominion cycle, you need first t value yourself as an employer and continue to see value in yourself on a daily basi It has to do with looking inside us and outside us. *After seeing value in yoursel you need to see value in the resources that God has put in the universe and thos on which man has added value on in the market place.* Seeing value in th resources is not enough. *The next step to make resources valuable is to add valu to the identified resources around you and beyond you that are aligned to yot competence.*

A combination of value addition on yourself and on the resources around you an beyond you is the starting point on your journey to dominion as an employe Fruitfulness has actually to deal with exploiting the value in us (the blessing, th potential) and adding that value on the resources around and beyond us. Th continuous value addition that contributes to improving the welfare of the customer is a key component in fruitfulness. What surrounds you as resources are the basis fc your going forward. This requires that you have eyes to see the resources you hav and the resources around you. Fruitfulness means that you get committed to addin more value to the value that you see in yourself and multiply that value. Further, yc add the multiplied value to resources around and transform them into products c services to be marketed to the world.

Value addition on yourself which we may call personal development is like fu that propels the engine of an aeroplane from a runway into the skies. The mor fruit you produce and the higher the value of that fruit, the higher its demand i the market place. When you increase your value that in turn adds value to th resources around you and beyond you and then multiply the value added, it move you to another level in the dominion cycle. The multiplied value will require that is distributed around the globe. I have pointed out that I read a write up on one sho in China to say the World is My Runway. What I deduced from the write up wa that the world is a runway from where you are. After taking off on a lifelong journe of fruitfulness leading to dominion, there has to be continuous value addition c yourself and on the resources around and beyond you.

While fruitfulness and multiplication are important, we may benefit little if we do not go to the next level in the dominion cycle called filling the earth or distribution of our multiplied fruit. This is a very important level if we have to see the impact from our products and services and influence the whole world with our products and services.

CHAPTER 13: DEVELOPING YOUR PRODUCT OR SERVICE TO TAKE TO THE MARKET

THE FIVE STAGES OF DEVELOPING A PRODUCT OR SERVICE

I have taught my family five stages to be taken towards developing a product/service. We used these stages in our coming up with the music products that we have put on the market. Given that we went through them well in advance, we were able to face the challenges we had with calmness, strength, courage and focus. *This gave us direction and focus on the results we wanted. We knew where we were going as we embarked on the vision to produce music that will be unique and superior to touch the whole world.* I have so far shared these stages with other people who have been provoked to go into spending time to think as they go through the five stages. *I call the product or service the thing for simplicity purpose.*

These five steps are:

- *DEFINE IT*
- *LOOK FOR IT*
- *FIND IT*
- *USE IT*
- *BENEFIT FROM IT*

DEFINING IT- *It is imperative that you first define the thing that you want to have. Define your vision before you start looking for the required resources to use to fulfil the vision.* Habakkuk 2:2 says that you need to define the thing; your vision by writing it and making it plain on tablets so that he may run who reads it. Making the vision plain on tablets is about defining your vision clearly so that the herald/ the runner who reads it runs with it. *Clarity with what you want to do is key in whatever you want to do.* Spend time thinking especially in this "busy world". I have observed people who do not have time to think about what they want to do. They always look busy but do not seem to be achieving much. *Vision clarity leads to clear strategic decisions being made in its implementation.* Vision clarity also results in the right steps being taken with focus and the energy required to fulfil the vision. It propels the reader of the vision into action.

SPEND TIME DEFINING THE IDEA-THINKING

In writing your vision and making it plain, there is an investment of time needed. We need to spend time incubating our ideas. For a chicken to produce a chick, it spends time incubating the egg. A human being baby goes through eight to nine months for it to be born. An elephant has a longer gestation period and definitely it produces something bigger. *I have told my family that if you want to produce a mosquito, the gestation period is shorter than when you want to produce an elephant. The more time you spend incubating your ideas as you develop them, the better are the outputs from your time investment.*

A JOURNEY ON DEFINING THE THING-THE IDEA, THE VISION

In my opinion, *I have come to believe that when you spend time in defining your idea clearly, you save a lot of future time, energy and money.* This is so because you will have used the defining process to help you seal certain loopholes or altogether decide to throw away the idea or sell it to another person. Remember *you were not born to implement all the ideas you end up having in this world because your time here on earth is limited. Concentrate on those areas where you have competitive advantage which will give you a sense of meaning and fulfilment.*

DEFINING YOUR THING: KEY PRODUCT OR SERVICE INITIAL DEVELOPMENT STEPS

The following are some of the key initial product development steps to be taken when developing your product. I led my family into applying these initial steps to our prototype music production as we ventured into gospel music singing:

- Define the objective for developing your product or service
- Spend time coming up with what you exactly want to do
- Clearly define what you want to do- defining the idea
- Define what you have in form of resources to be used to produce the thing/product/service
- Clearly know the form in which you will produce and package your product/service
- Define your niche (your share of market) before you venture into product development. Remember not everybody is your customer or fan. Not everyone will cheer you up because there are many of you to be cheered up. So the others could be cheering your friends. Remember your niche is your wealth.
- Get business consultancy from the Holy Spirit to guide you into all truth (Isaiah30:21, John 16:21). The Holy Spirit knows the mind of God (1 Corinthians2:11). *The same God who was interested in Jacob's business affair with Laban is the same God yesterday, today*

and forever (Hebrews13:8). He made Jacob have a business turnaround and made him rich. He can give you business wisdom to carry out the decisions you need to make.
- *Listen to the voice of God before sowing a seed with the potential to give you a hundredfold like was the case with Isaac* (Genesis26:1-13). He listened to God who guided him regarding the right place in which to dwell at that right time and did a right thing by sowing a seed in the midst of famine.
- As a business person, *you require wisdom in order to build a business and take it in the right direction.* You can draw from Proverbs24:3 which says that by wisdom a house is built. *You can use wisdom as well to build a business.*
- Define the stakeholders in producing the thing/product. Since you are undertaking a project, it is important that you clearly define who your stakeholders are in having the thing come into being. These may include employees, suppliers of raw materials and your partners in the business undertaking.
- Define the product/service that you want to offer on the market
- Define the ingredients of the product/service .Define the ingredients (what materials/ resources will be combined/ mixed to produce the product/service)
- Define the package(the container/ the jar / the carrier of the product)
- Define the content (what will the container/package carry)
- Establish the other resources required in producing your product or your service
- Establish the cost of production in coming up with the product or service.
- Define your target group/ customers. *Whatever you produce is supposed to be distributed to the consumers who are your target group or your customers.* It is one thing to spend resources on production and another thing to have what has been produced sold out to customers. In this regard, it is important that from the very beginning you define who your buyers are so that you do not get stranded with your thing (your product). *Marketing your thing (product) then is key to the success of your business.* It is this component that seals what the third business law called filling the earth requires.
- Define the heralds/ the runners (Hab2:2)-*Define the human capital to be used in the production, marketing and selling of the product/service.* Heralds play an important role in making sure that a thing (a product) is announced to customers. Expertise in marketing is required to have the product sold to customers.

To me, I believe that *the aspect of definition is the most important stage. The majority of people avoid this stage or try to do it on the surface and rush into looking for a thing.* This has been one of the failures of the initiatives people undertake. *It is important that we define the product or service that we want before we start looking or searching for it.*

DEFINING OUR PRODUCTS AND SERVICES

One day my daughter Jireh came to tell me that she wanted to implement a particular program and wanted a discussion with me. I reminded her of the five stages of product development that I have developed and communicated to her (Define it, Look for it, Find it and Use it, Benefit from it) that I had taught them. It is good that she was able to recall 3 of them and I reminded her of the other two. We then embarked on a journey to product development and what we came up with was a mind opener. I then shared the same with others and I concluded that this was a key process people needed to go through especially defining the thing. As I have already pointed out, you will realize that the majority of people rarely define what they want to do. They instead rush into looking for things to do which they take into implementation that turn out to be project failure.

By the way as, we discussed, Jireh actually told me that she wanted to overtake me with what she wanted to do. I told her that I was happy for her to tell me that because that is what we parents should be looking forward to. *We parents have to reach a stage where, like Jacob in the Bible, we go into the background so that our sons go in the forefront and implement our* **ideas.** Remember it is our sons who are supposed to contend with our enemies at the gate according to Psalms127:3-5.

In this regard, I was very excited as she pointed out what we had and what it takes if we defined clearly what will enable us to sell our products and services to the market. We did an audit of what we had as capital as follows: Her story regarding her getting into University without mathematics and science, My story, the music, teachings say on the employer in you and other potential products and services and many more. We realized that we had a lot with us to establish ourselves as employers.

LOOKING FOR IT AFTER THE DEFINITION

What you will have done at the defining level is actually an element of strategic planning. After going through the defining process of the thing or the product or service you want, you now have to look for it. You have up to this point defined what to do. You have defined your product; your fruit. You now have to venture into looking for what you have expectations for in order to ultimately expect to find it. ***Defining your product and getting the needed details about it will help you when you come to looking for it. It will also prevent you to avoid taking decisions hastily without planning. Further it will help you minimize bumping into thieves who may want to steal from you, even kill you and destroy you or kill your dream about the product you are looking for.*** At the time of definition, it is expected that you will have gathered the necessary information regarding the type of market you are venturing into looking for your product. Please gather as much information as possible for use in looking for the type of product you are venturing into. Take risks but they should be risks based on information. Don't give the devil a chance to destabilize your plans. So gather the required necessary information.

I remember when we were getting into gospel music with my family, we did not know where to start from and where to end. What we had was the desire to get in singing especially with my daughter Jireh having initially come up with the idea to come up with a gospel music album. I made her and the other members of the family to go into the defining process so as to make it clear about what we wanted to achieve.

We then asked ourselves where the components of what we were looking for could be found. This made us get into research and finally we identified the various components and where we were to find them. We then started looking for the components so that we could assemble them together to finally have the product that we wanted. The initial decision was to practice the singing of the songs, improve them and then engage someone to record the music. During the recording we got some disappointments, which of course you expect, as you go looking or searching for what you want. Despite the challenges, especially after having defined the thing we wanted, we ended up having the first album ever in the name of my daughter Jireh. The next was for us to venture into having a video for the songs, which we also had never done before. We managed to have a video for the eight songs for Jireh. ***I challenged my family to think and design the video ourselves contrary to their thinking that we needed to take the designing to experts. My aim was to make them realize the great potential for them to think and design something they have never done before.*** The good news is that they managed to do it with my guidance.

Remember that we were cognizant of making mistakes while learning. While we did not want to compromise standards, we were also aware of the enemy called perfection whereby wanting to perfect things make you fail to take any product to the market. Of course the Bible in 2 Corinthians 13:11 tells us to aim for perfection but wanting to perfect should not prevent us from taking a product or service to the market when it has reached a reasonable consumption level. That is why there are what are called editions, versions, levels and so forth. This allows for improvement in our product or service development. In this regard then, we tried to put the product on the market and we were overwhelmed with the positive response from most of the people who listened to Jireh's music. This gave us courage and encouragement to promote our gospel music further in terms of product development. We went a step further to have a music studio in our home where my nephew had to learn from the scratch how to produce music.

At a given point I also started singing, since in the earlier production I simply wrote two of the songs and gave guidance to the other six songs. At the time of this writing, I had also produced a gospel music album which is now on the market. This music was composed, arranged and produced in my home. *What fulfilment and meaning I had derived resulting from this!*

FINDING IT

The Bible in Matthew7:7 says seek and you will find. The principle here is that when we venture into seeking something, the chances are that we end up finding it. What this means is that we need to have the expectation of finding what we are seeking, especially when we undertake to define what we want to look for first. Ecclasiastes9:10 talks about you finding something to do. It says whatsoever your hand finds to do, you have to put in your best in terms of your thoughts (planning), ideas (knowledge), skills (wisdom) to work out whatsoever your hand has found to do. So then *finding is a very important component in venturing into product development.*

GOING INTO INCUBATION OF YOUR IDEAS FOR PRODUCT OR SERVICE DEVELOPMENT AFTER FINDING WHAT TO DO

The Bible in Genesis1:1 tells us that when God created the heavens and the earth, the earth was without form, empty (void) and darkness covered the surface of the deep. What I like out of this narration is the statement that the Spirit of God was hovering over the surface of the waters. This precedes verse 3 of Genesis 1.When the Bible tells us that the Spirit of God hovered this was incubation before God started making from the earth what He ended up making. *The making of all what followed up the creation and making process was preceded by incubation.*

The process from conception to delivering of a specie is called, in biology, gestation period. *Many of us depending on the type of specie we need to produce will have different 'gestation' periods. Despite having different gestation periods, what is key is that it is time we produced the specie we were created to produce.* Many of us have been carrying some "pregnancies" for a long time. These pregnancies need not be aborted but delivered to benefit society. *A specie needs to be given birth from our 'wombs' and deployed to the market so that we become a blessing to our audience.*

THE ENEMY CALLED PERFECTION

As we have pointed out above, 2Corinthians13:11 tells us to aim for perfection. What this means is that you start from somewhere and find yourself somewhere- on top. *Many of us have failed to bring up something we have perceived in our minds because we want them to start in their perfect state.* This is not how God created the earth. The earth moved from imperfection to perfection. We are told in Genesis1:1-2, that in the beginning when the heavens and the earth were created the earth was formless, empty and darkness covered the surface of the waters. The promising thing in this was that the Spirit of God was hovering over the surface of the deep. This meant that something good was being incubated or brooded upon. What follows from verse 3 to verse 31 of Genesis1 was perfecting the creation by each day adding value to the creation. *God aimed for perfecting His creation as He labelled what He made each day with a 'good' until He finally labelled the sum total of His creation and making with a 'very good' label.* This is a demonstration of making progress from formlessness, emptiness and darkness to where a very good conclusion was made leading to God resting on the seventh day. The resting by God was after the excellent works that He had done.

USING IT

The essence of defining the thing followed by looking for it and finding it is that you want to utilize it when you find it. It means that you have placed value on the thing before you look for it. After finding it, utilization of the thing is the basis for looking for it. *The things you seek in life are those which you as an individual or a society has placed value on.* It is the placing of value on the thing that makes them place a value on it in order to acquire it. This is called, in economics, the willingness to pay for that thing. Since value will have been placed on the thing, you price it. Given the willingness to pay by those demanding your product, people in the market purchase the thing resulting from them placing value to it. *Remember that life is about exchange of what you have with what another has.* Since we have to go into exchange which is called trade, we have to undertake the following in order for us to get the best from the exchange in the trade:

DECIDE AND ENDEAVOUR TO MAKE YOUR PRODUCT OR SERVICE UNIQUE AND SUPERIOR

Decide and endeavour to make your product unique and superior. This is what makes customers look for your product/service. Do not specialize in imitating but specialize in innovation and creativity. To me the difference between imitation and innovation is that imitation is a complete copying what has already been done while innovation means improving what has already been done. At one point as we were developing gospel music, I told one of my daughters that we needed to make our music unique in terms of content and packaging the songs. I said that it is not helpful to doing things exactly the way everybody has done it or is doing it. This dawned on my mind more than ever when someone took me to a hotel where he spent money to buy me and another colleague some meal.

Before we went to the hotel, I tried to persuade the person that we needed to go to a cheaper place for him to save. But because he needed a unique product, he insisted he we needed to go to that hotel because disturbances were limited there. So the reason why the person was willing to pay a higher price was that the hotel had a unique and superior brand compared to the cheaper place I was suggesting to go to.

At the end of our discussion, *a strong feeling dawned on my mind that I had a unique and superior brand for the person to take me to that hotel.* This was after my seeing the excitement on his face and the feedback he gave me regarding the fact that the sharing I had with him and the other person we were with made them see something unique that they needed to go and look at further. *The impression about the uniqueness of what I had become stronger when I got home and my wife told me that someone I previously had a talk with wanted me to speak to her further on the subject I had shared with her. Now I am convinced I have a unique and superior brand to market to the whole world.*

PACKAGING YOUR PRODUCT

I have been encouraging some of the people to realize the talents, skills and experience in them that are dormant to deliberately start packaging their products and services before finding the place to use them. *I personally got an encouragement from David in the Bible who packaged his experience of killing lions and bears as potential experience to be utilized in a military setup.* This gives us a classic example of transfer of knowledge from killing lions and bears to killing Goliath. With this understanding, I also have started packaging the products and services that I realized I have. *I have been packaging products and services from my vast working experience, my skills, talents and knowledge by adding value to them.* The packaging of what I have has really paid off to date.

The result of packaging what I have made me find myself giving a motivation talk to a gathering of Permanent Secretaries for the Zambian Government chaired by the Country's Secretary to Cabinet. This was a self-actualization encounter where I spoke in this manner at a high level forum for the first time in my life. After speaking, a number of Permanent Secretaries came to appreciate me for the motivation talk on the need for them to reposition themselves to the new approach to planning. This was followed by a speech I gave in China where I went for a course in March, 2017. I was among four people who were asked to give speeches on behalf of about 238 people comprising participants from different countries. After giving my speech, the Master of Ceremony commented that my speech was full of energy and told me that they would publish it in the Chinese Media. *As I read the speech, I saw the audience clapping after moving them with my speech on the leadership trajectory as a variable for development.* Afterwards many people came to congratulate me. Some of them got the copy of the speech of which one of the participants who owns a Newspaper in Lesotho went to use my speech as a headline in his Newspaper and entitled the headline as: Simon Kayekesi Leadership Trajectory for the Emancipation of Lesotho. When he sent me the newspaper page and I read it, *I realized the giant who was in me but lying idle in the four corners of an office as an employee instead of being an employer. It motivated me to realize that my product could be read in a country I had never been to* and yet I had gone there with my packaged product. *What an inspiration this has been to me ever since!*

What I learnt from this is that packaging your products and services is a preparation that creates room for you to find yourself in the presence of great men and women. I am now looking forward to having many more as I have continued packaging my products. I urge you also to start packaging your products and services in readiness for the day when some customer(s) will demand for them. If you have already started, I encourage you to continue and multiply your fruit to give you the desired results. At the beginning, the results you get may not be encouraging but by faith you can believe that your efforts will one day pay off. For example Joseph, in the Bible, continued packaging his product while in prison waiting for a day when Pharaoh would have a dream. Since he was ready with the ability to interpret dreams, he went to deliver when he was called without saying first give me time to prepare. The result was his release from prison to be part of the Egyptian leadership. *It pays to package what you have in readiness for would be customers.* Someone has said that it is better to be prepared for an opportunity than not preparing and then you find the opportunity. Please prepare yourself for that opportunity to come your way.

BRANDING YOUR PRODUCT

Brand your product/service with a brand that will make customers have a perceived high value of your product. When God created and made you he placed a brand on you. You then use the brand on you to come up with your branded product. It is that brand on you that you use to place value on your product which makes people place a high value on your product. ***Despite God's brand on us, many of us are culprits of rebranding ourselves according to the patterns of this world and resulting in the loss the originality in us.*** This is because of the society we find ourselves in which places on us false impressions. But it is cardinal if we have to benefit from our products if in the same way God branded you and me, ***we brand our products/services with the uniqueness they deserve as we take them to the market.***

BENEFITING FROM THE THING (THE PRODUCT)

The major reason for utilizing a thing that you sought and found after defining it is to derive benefits from it. Remember you started by defining clearly what you wanted. In this regard, you came up with a vision to have the thing. You started by visualizing your product being in its finished state. You then developed a master plan for you to look for or seek the thing. The result was that you found the thing which led to you utilizing it. ***The ultimate reason for going through the four steps was for you to benefit from utilizing the thing.*** The benefits are in various forms. For example, the benefits may be inform of profits or having the control over a particular thing that you seek. These may also simply be praise from people or satisfaction and self-fulfilment. That is why we get disappointed after getting a thing and we fail to derive the perceived benefits from it.

Benefits are, therefore, key in the whole process of product development as the ultimate. That is why it is important from the very beginning to define the thing and undertake a process mapping for getting the thing and utilizing it to get the required benefits. Les Brown says you need to look at yourself; make it important that you find somewhere to use your talents and gifts to generate the income that allows you to control your destiny. He quotes what he read which said you either control your destiny or someone else will.

THE PRINCIPLE OF MULTIPLYING YOUR PRODUCT TO BENEFIT FROM IT

You need to multiply your product if you have to benefit from it. This multiplication is designed by God for your prosperity. There is a secret or mystery in the potential in your seed or product to sprout into a plant and bear fruit. As a seed sower you expect your seed to sprout as a result of the investment and go into multiplying your seed sown. This principle comes out in 2Corinthians9:10 where God is said to be a seed supplier and you being the sower. ***The purpose of sowing seed is its multiplication. It is the increased harvest that increases your prosperity or wealth accumulation.*** In Mark 4:26-29, the mystery in the growth of a plant spouting from sown seed to being a tree is presented as follows:

1. There someone to sow the seed (the capital)
2. There has to be a ground on which the seed has to be sown (the earth, a human being, an investment sector, an arena).
3. When seed is sown, you may go to sleep after watering, weeding and fertilizing it because it has in itself the potential to sprout. And there is one who makes the plant to grow -God. (1 Corinthians 3:6-7).
4. The growth of a plant is a mystery. You can understand the biology but you cannot really comprehend how the growth itself takes place.

As can be seen from the above illustration from Mark4:26-29, seed has a process through which it has to go for it to ripen and be harvested. This is further illustrated in the diagram below to demonstrate how the earth goes through a seed sprouting and fruit production process. This starts with the seed being sown in the earth. When seed receives rain, it sprouts into a plant. The plant is designed in such a way that it has potential to bear fruit carrying in it seed. The seed gets into the ground from which more plants sprouts and finally you have a forest with plenty of fruit from the plants. This ensures continuity in the type of seed, the type of fruit and the type of plant. When you gain understanding on this, it will make you attach great importance in seeing to it that your fruit is multiplied.

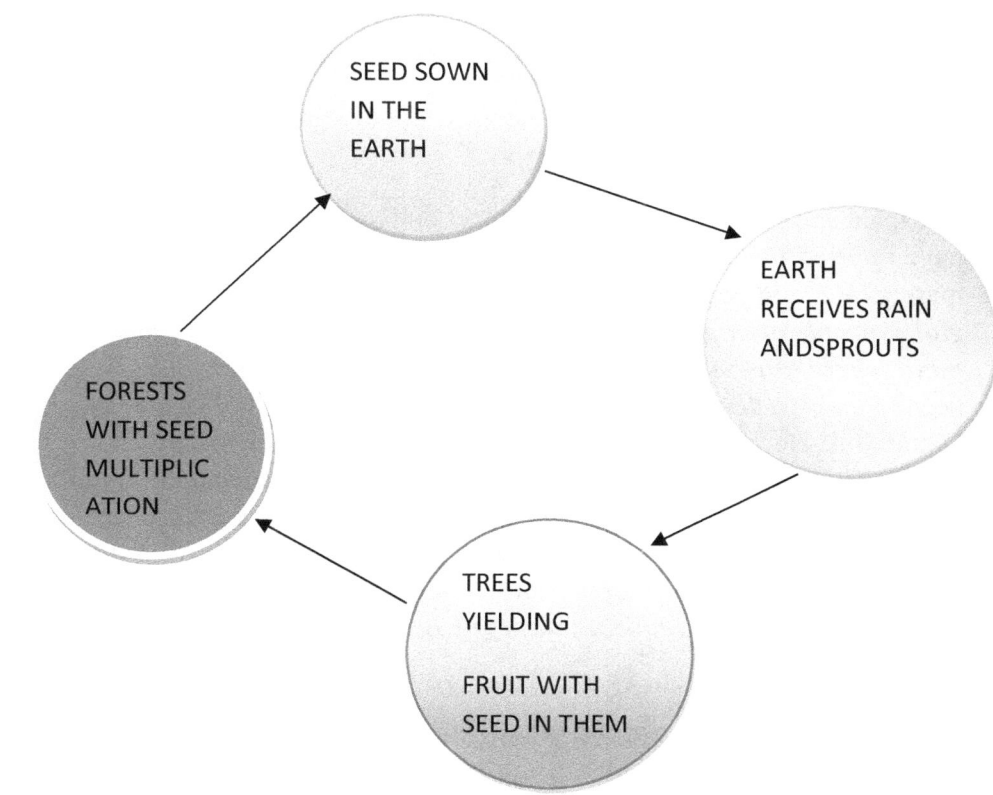

FIGURE 7: THE CYCLE FOR FRUITFULNESS FROM SOWN SEED

In a similar manner to this illustration, because you were formed from the earth and God breathed into you and you become a living soul, you have something in you similar to the earth. You have the ability to produce fruit from the seed implanted in you by God. Like the earth that sprouts plants when it receives rain, you also sprout when you receive the word of God in your heart. The earth produces all by itself because it has potential to sprout. *You also in the same way can produce by yourself because you have potential to produce. You can sprout the seed sown and make others start harvesting from your fruit-your product.*

CHAPTER 14: MARKETING YOUR PRODUCT OR FRUIT

YOU ARE A GLOBAL BEING

The main speaker at the Winners' Chapel on Kingdom Entrepreneurship that I have referred to above pointed out that you and I are designed for the global market. *He said you and I are on Jesus' organizational Chart and we are global people of impact.* He then said that *you need to have a global vision in mind where you see yourself as a kingdom entrepreneur.* He said all you need to do is to *develop and turn your talent into skill* like Joseph, David and Daniel did. He also said that you need to believe in the manufacturer-Jesus Christ. *You need to use your brain which is the greatest capital and that you need business wisdom.* You also need to take some risks that can lead to rewards. He said the following: *"I am afraid of myself-doing what I have never done in life and seeing what I have never seen before." These are some of the secrets to realizing what you are already-a global being.*

YOU ARE A GLOBAL MARKETER

You are designed by God to be a global marketer. I have come to understand global marketing more with the internet being in place and the media in general being in place. *You can be connected to millions of clients or customers all over the world at a goal because of information, communication and technology.* You as one carrying a dominion blessing already in you are intended to market your fruit to the globe. You are a global marketer. Remember God blessing man and saying to man to be fruitful, multiply, fill the earth and subdue it in order to dominate. Look at God emphasizing the dominion mandate to Noah according to His original intention in Genesis1:26-28. In order to emphasize the mandate, God put His blessing on Noah and commanded him to become fruitful, to multiply and to teem in the earth (to distribute his fruit) in the earth as stated in Genesis9:3, 7. *What God had in mind for Noah was the globe. What God has for you and me is the globe. We thank God for us to live during the era of globalization and technology.* No wonder, the world is getting more connected than ever before especially through information, communication and technology (ICT). *Business can now be done on a screen of a computer or a phone in one's palm!*

I am reminded of the first car that I ever owned. I bought it from the internet. What a wonderful era in which we are in for us to utilize the dominion mandate as we go through the dominion cycle.

God told Noah that into his hand was delivered the resources which Noah had with him in the ark. Even *you and I have within us and around us resources from God at our disposal.* God told Noah that He was giving him everything that He needed. *He told Noah that resources were delivered into his hand to make sure that he utilized them to his advantage. It was up to Noah to take advantage of what God gave him with his family by going through the dominion cycle of fruitfulness, multiplication, distribution and subduing so as to dominate.* It was up to Noah to squander or to get the best out of the available resources. That is why 2Peter1:3-4 is always provoking me to note that God's divine nature has given me everything I need for life and godliness. I am then the one to blame for the state in which I am because as far as God is concerned He has already done His part. What you see from the very beginning in the dominion cycle is that man had to go through it to realize his dominion mandate. This idea is emphasized in Noah and in Abraham. The theme goes through scripture into the New Testament. It is the theme of fruitfulness, multiplication, distribution and subduing leading to dominion. Each one of us is required to go through the dominion cycle if we are to dominate here on earth. We are all carrying a dominion gene within us.

And our arena for domination is the earth.

As I have already pointed out, while driving through one of the Chinese cities called Chongqing, I read a write-up on one of the shops which said that the world is my runway. This part of the write-up was done on the day of my arrival from China. I had travelled by air from Lusaka to Beijing, China. From Beijing, I went to the airport and flew to a city called Chongqing after which I flew to Shanghai and back to Beijing and then I flew back to Zambia. In all cases the aeroplanes used a runway before take-off and for landing. All the points used acted as points for my take off and as spring boards for me to get to locations I had never been to before. This shows how *we are now able to move round the global and that the world (the globe) is our runway. The earth is your global market. You are actually a global marketer.*

YOUR BUSINESS SHOULD HAVE A GLOBAL PERSPECTIVE BY APPLYING THE DISTRIBUTION PRINCIPLE AND MAKE YOU BENEFIT FROM YOUR PRODUCT

In Matthew28:19-20, we see Jesus being global minded. He talked of the disciples going to all the parts of the world. In Acts1:8, Jesus talked of Jerusalem, Samaria, Judea and the uttermost parts of the world. This is how far He envisaged His Gospel Business impact to reach. *At least the minimum your business impact should go is outside your house or your heart to impact a neighbour.* Thank God that among the courses that I have done is called Global issues in entrepreneurship. *This requires that we have a global mind for undertaking business if we have to benefit from globalization. This will help us to venture into the unexploited global market for our unique products and services.*

DEPLOY YOURSELF: YOU HAVE AN AUDIENCE LOOKING FOR YOUR VALUE-DONT LET THEM DOWN.

There are people out there who you have not yet connected to who have been looking for the treasure you carry- your product. These people are yet to find you. Since you were in your mother's womb, there was an audience waiting for you to be born. Your mother and father could have been the first category of the audience including the midwives who welcomed you when you were born. Ever since, there has always been an audience waiting for you as God's masterpiece to display God's splendor in you to your audience. That audience has been yearning the gifting the abilities and the talents endowed in you as you exploit the potential in you.

Whether it is in area like football, politics, education, music and other fields there is always an audience waiting for you to come out. Some of them are still looking for you and are yet to meet you. Many of us have had an audience or fans that have been looking for us all the years we have been on earth. They are actually waiting for you and me. *You and I have our audiences respectively whom we are meant to attend to. None of us is without a fan or a customer out there.* For example you may be having laughing fans or customers whom your comedy can supply by making them pay you for making them laugh. There are many opportunities out there since given the variety of customers in the global from which you have your share of customers called a niche.

LET YOUR LIGHT SHINE

One day I was praying to God to enlarge my territory based on my dream song which I mentioned above. I got a strong impression that all I needed to do was to let my light shine according to Mattthew5:14. *As I shine my customers, like insects get attracted to light, get attracted to my light. In turn, I influence them with my product until I get customer loyalty. By continuously shining and making my light shine more and farther, I will ultimately enlarge my territory when my area of influence expands.*

There is no better way to deploy yourself than to start shining. In so doing, you will end up having a share of the market of people who get attracted to your light. The aspect of shining by putting your lamp on top was illuminated fully in my heart when my grandson Perez, as he was playing, put the lamp under the bed while I was on the bed while editing this book. The main bulb in the bedroom was off. Since I did not take note of the action he had taken, I only discovered as it was getting dark that *there were some rays of light across the room but the room was not fully lit.* When I checked, I realized that *he had put the lamp below the bed while it was on*. Immediately what Jesus said that you do not light a lamp and put it under the table but *put it on top so that it shines in the whole room dawned on me strongly. I then related it to the discussion of you and I being global marketers. For you and me to reach out to that audience that we were born to serve, we need to shine so that they can be drawn to our light and make them benefit from it.*

We have already pointed out above that in Genesis8:22, there are always consumers or buyers of a good or service. *This means that there is always a need for a supplier or seller of the goods and services being demanded.* You then are not just a potential consumer on demand side but you are also a potential supplier of some products or services. *You are a potential seller as opposed to being simply a potential buyer. Individuals or nations that are net buyers instead of being net sellers end up in poverty. You need to be a net seller where you end up having surplus instead of living in deficit.* At any given point, you are either on the side of consumers (buyers) or you are on the side of suppliers (sellers). What is clear is that *fewer people are on the suppliers' side (sellers) compared to the bigger number on the side of consumers (buyers)*. Because they are fewer, *suppliers (sellers) of a commodities normally tend to put more money into their pockets, especially entrepreneurs, than the net buyers who include employees.*

Employees, like the other net buyers in the market, ultimately get peanuts in this supply and demand chain. Remember employees simply supply labor compared to the entrepreneurs who deploy their capital into the supply and demand chain. This capital can themselves as human capital, or financial capital or social capital like trust. *The principle is that the laborer is due his or her wages. He or she is not due his dividends. It is the employer who is due his or her dividends.*

HAVING AN AWARENESS OF YOUR NICHE

As we have established so far, *there is what is called a niche. Your niche` is your share of market.* This is a share of the market which you have control over in terms of the demand for your products. *Your niche is your wealth.* There is need to have an awareness of your niche and establish how to manage them for them to continue purchasing your product. *All you need to do is to first and foremost have an awareness of a group of people out there who have been looking for you all along but are yet to locate you.* As we have pointed out, we thank God for what internet and the media in general can do for you and me.

To shed more light on your audience looking for let me share with you my experience. I was looking for a man, for a number of years, whose tape message I had listened to and learned a lot from. His sharing had helped me to appreciate certain things that made me want to meet him. One day I met the man when an opportunity had availed itself. *Time to be connected to this man had come. I met the man and greeted him after being introduced to him but it did not dawn on me that this was the man I had been looking for.* We moved to some other place together but it never came to my mind that I had found the man I was looking for. But an occasion came when we sat at the same table at the guest house where we were staying. As we talked he said something which came to me like a revelation and I concluded that this was the man I had been looking for a number of years. I narrated to him how much I had learnt from his message and how I was able to quote some of his statements. From that day, I got connected to the man who also ended up benefiting from what I was carrying.

So, as we have pointed out above, be aware that though you have not yet met them, you have some people looking for you. Having this awareness will help you start preparing yourself to meet your audience. In doing this, you need to have an insight into what your audience would like to see in you or to get from you. *Start taking actions that will lead to your developing the products or services that your audience is looking for from you.*

So then put it in your mind that your category of the audience whom you may also call customers have been searching for you ever since. Once again, it is important for you to understand the market by undertaking research and appreciating what your category of customers want. *In some cases, you may not exactly know who these customers are and may not know what they are looking for. You, however, should engage yourself in designing your product or service by perceiving what your customers could be looking for. Your produce will then have to be taken to the market by making sure that your customers perceive that your product is of superior value.* By you doing so, you will then find some customers who when they taste your products or services will be drawn to them. This is because it will have met a need they have had for many years even when they did not consciously know about the need.

The key then is having an awareness of our potential buyers or consumers out there and venturing into product or service development. We should always remember that our audience or customers are looking for quality products or services. However, while upholding the importance of quality products or services, we should, as we have pointed out above, beware of waiting to perfect things forever before taking them to the market. *What I have learnt so far is that product or service development goes through a growth phase.* That is why the Japanese have used the Kaizen Concept which implies making incremental improvements on our products or services. *As you go on with product or service development, you need to reach a point where, after putting in all the effort, you have to make a decision to take your product or service on the market.* You do this while not giving up on improving it. Although there is a saying that the first cut is the deepest, it may only be true to some extent but it may not hold for each and every case. *The depth of the cut may depend on a number of factors among them the sharpness of the tool being used. At the same time it also depends on how hard or soft what is being cut is. There is still room for you to improve your quality in case the first one (the first cut) was not very good.*

So then *when you have an idea it may go through creating phases in order for it to reach a level at which it can be of a higher standard than when you first put it on the market.* No wonder you have versions or editions or new packaging of the products or services. The state of the product or service at beginning may not have the form according to the required standard. But by making improvements on the product or service, it reaches a point where the product or service will have a higher value than at the beginning. This can be seen in God's creation and making process as written in Genesis 1 and as we have already established above. *God produced the product called earth and He went on in the six days to add form on the earth and populating it with things to make it wonderful.* He went on evaluating His products and went on labelling them as good until He looked at the overall work which included the creation of the man and concluded with the words, "Very good " (Genesis 1:31).

YOUR NICHE IS YOUR WEALTH

Let me share with you the application of the idea of a niche to coming up with my products. As I was thinking about coming about with a company name I came up with **PEREZWECA** as my main business name with its subsidiaries.

The name may change but the most important thing is the insight I gained on what I am capable of binging out from my mind with a niche is mind. The following is what I wrote as my business logo as I thought and imagined in my mind.

FIGURE 8: PEREZWECA BUSINESS LOGO

What was so inspiring was for me to come up with such a piece of art from my mind given my level of competence in this area. *The question I asked myself was: Is it true that I am the one who has done this? It made me realize that I have something which I can produce and there is a share of the market that comprise my wealth.* Therefore in designing our company, I came up with this statement: *Our niche is our wealth.* This gives us focus on our cust*omers the share of the market which we have acquired and are yet to acquire.* Part of the niche are those customers you already have but you also have those you have not yet met. So as we have established be aware that though you have not yet met them, you have some people looking for your product. After having this awareness, *start preparing yourself to meet your audience-your customers*. Again as pointed out above, in doing this, you need to have an insight into what your audience, your customers, would like to see in you or to get from you. *Have you started taking actions that will lead to your developing the products or services that your audience is looking for?*

CLAIM YOUR SHARE OF THE PIE WITH YOUR PRODUCT.

Look at the diagram below depicting a pie with your share of the pie in the earth.

FIGURE8: YOUR SHARE OF THE WORLD MARKET OF YOUR

PRODUCT

The pie can be a representation of the earth in which God put the resources. You have the share in the resources of the earth. Psalms24:1 says that the earth is God's and the fullness therefore. Now Psalms115:16 says that the heavens belong to the Lord and the earth which is His, He has given to the sons of men. So in essence God leased the earth to you. You are among the sons of men. So you are a shareholder of the earth and its resources. What is your share of the earth's resources? *How much of the share of the earth's resources that you get will depend to a large extent on the position you take in the earth and what you will do while in that position. You know, what God put in the earth is like a pie with you having a share. It is up to you to claim the share of your pie.* We have already alluded to the fact that God as we are told in 2 Peter1:3-4 has given you and me all we need for life and for godliness. I Timothy6:17 tells us that God gives us everything to enjoy. What is this everything?

It is like the principle of per capital in economics. Per capital is derived from dividing the population into the measure that is being considered in order to know how much each individual is supposed to get. For example, *the per capital income of a nation means that is the share of the nation's wealth that an individual citizen is entitled if the wealth of that nation was to be shared equally.* For various reasons, some individuals end up getting more than what others get. And as we have already established 3 percent of the population get 97 percent of the world's share of wealth. You may comfort yourself by saying that a number of those comprising the 3 percent get wealth selfishly through stealing and corruption. You may be right. *But let us look at entrepreneurs, the ones I have termed employers which is the subject of this book. You will agree with me that they have done what you and I may have not done and may possibly not be willing to do. They take risks which you and I may have not taken and may not be willing to take.* They take the position of the employer which you and I may have not taken and may not be willing to take at all. *Do you expect the same results as those of an employer or an entrepreneur if you have not taken up the place of an employer or are not willing to?* The obvious answer is a big NO. This is where the difference is. It is in the position you take either as an employee or an employer. *That is why this book is about repositioning your mind from having an employee mind to having an employer mind. It is about you having a paradigm shift that will take you into a new position- the position of an employer.* You then embark on the journey of joining the 3 percent who enjoy 97 percent of the world's wealth.

MARKETING YOUR FRUIT; YOUR PRODUCT AS AN EMPLOYER

At this point I take it that you have repositioned your mind by transforming yourself into having an employer mind. And I take it that now you have made a decision to become an employer to produce your fruit to market to the world. *It is now your responsibility to produce your fruit, multiply it, market it and move towards subduing with your fruit and ultimately have dominion as an employer.* If you are already on the employer side, I take it that these insights have added more insights to what you already have towards enhancing your fruitfulness and having dominion on earth. What remains for you now is to venture your multiplied fruit. *Make sure that you sustain what you have become as a result of repositioning yourself and become what God made you to be and called you to be.*

CONCLUSION

We have come to the conclusion of this series on *The Employer in You: Repositioning Yourself from Having an Employee Mind to Having an Employer Mind.* I trust that transformation has taken place in your mind awaiting to bring out its outcomes for you as you release the employer in you. The next series of the Employer in You will go a step further to explain the elements that will make you consolidate your new position as an employer. This will give you a sense of fulfilment in life so that you really become what you were made to be-an employer.
God bless you.

1. Haggai E.D. 2009, **The Influential leader: 12 Steps to Igniting Visionary Decision Making,** Harvest Publishers, Eugene,

2. www.thefreedictionary.com/repositioning,

3. **Wolcott and Lippitz, Definition of corporate entrepreneurship**, www.seipa.edu.pl

4. Hill. N, (2005), **The Master Key to Riches, 21st Century** Edition, Manjul Publishing, New Delhi.

5. John Gills Salem Web Network Commentary, "**The four things a man should do according to the Jews**"

6. Robert. T, Kiyosaki etal, 2010, **The Business of the 21st Century**, Dream builders, Lake Dallas

7. Robert. T, Kiyosaki. 2012, **Before You Quit Your Job: 10 Real Life Lessons Every Entrepreneur Must Learn, Plata LLC** Publishing, Avenel

8. Jim Rohn. "**The Market Place pays for value**", www.youtube.com/watch?v=jnbdnkkceZw

9. www.fox news.com/us/2015/06/03/10

10. Wolcott and Lippitz on www.seipa.edu.pl

11. Jack Ma, **on opportunity**, www.youtube.com/watch?v=BUIEQyEtvmw.

12. Peter F. Drucker, 2005, **Innovation and Entrepreneurship: Practice Principles**, Routledge, London

13. Bob Proctor **on paradigms**,www.youtube.com/watch?v=z2IEiym_1Ym&t=99s

14. Munroe M. (1996), Maximizing **Your Potential: The Keys To Dying Empty,** Destiny Image Publishers, Shippensburg

15. Munroe M. **Regarding a job and work and entrepreneurship**, https://www.youtube.com/watch?v=j6fiY8IGpQY

16. Stevenson **on business meaning** http://kalyan-city.blogspot.com/2011/03/what-is-business-meaning-definitions.html http://kalyan-city.blogspot.com/2011/03/what-is-business-meaning-definitions.html

17. Lewis Henry **on business definition** http://kalyan-city.blogspot.com/2011/03/what-is-business-meaning-definitions.html http://kalyan-city.blogspot.com/2011/03/what-is-business-meaning-definitions.html

18. Ashimolowo Matthew **Raising Capacity an indication of our under achievement** on Kingsway International Christian Centre Television

19. Mike Murdock **on your decisions determining your wealth**, https://www.youtube.com/watch?v=mBGQ0oFh-Zo

20. Abioyemie D, on **knowing how to think and knowing why you should think**, the hour of salvation, Kingsway International Christian Centre Television

21. Pastor Bill Winston, **on attitude having to do with the altitude you go to**, on Kingsway International Christian Centre Television

22. Pastor Sam Adeyemi, **on undertaking some stock taking of what he had,** Success Power, Kingsway International Christian Centre Television

THE EMPLOYER IN YOU: REPOSITIONING YOURSELF FROM HAVING AN EMPLOYEE MIND TO HAVING AN EMPLOYER MIND

Trapped inside each one of us is an employer yearning to be released. There is an employer in you yearning to be released from an employee trap.

God made us employers. But alas, many of us end up being employees without realizing the employer in us that God made us to be. We find ourselves, as the late Man of God Myles Munroe put it, doing jobs we do not enjoy for the sake of a salary or a wage. Even for those who enjoy their jobs, most of them are in such jobs simply for sustenance. They spend most of their lives working hard to end up getting little compared to what they would have got if say they were employers.

Each one of us is carrying a "child" called an employer inside us waiting to be given birth to or we die with that child in us .The secret to giving birth to this child is in repositioning yourself from having an employee mind to having an employer mind.

In this first series, with many more to come on the Employer In You, you will, among other things, discover how it worked out for Jacob in the enterprise for Laban as recorded in Genesis30:25-43 & Genesis 31. If you apply the same principles Jacob used, you can see turnaround in your economic situation.

Simon Mbuyi Kayekesi, lives in Lusaka, Zambia. Having started as a teacher with a diploma in mathematics, he pursued the academic route and got an advanced Diploma in mathematics, then pursued a Degree in Economics and public Administration and later got a Masters in Economic Policy Management. He is now about to get a Doctorate in Business Administration. Despite what he considers a lot of investment academically and professionally, this has not translated into economic wellbeing. He has observed on the other side of the world

people with less education than him becoming economically sound. His study of the Bible in Genesis30:25-43 and Genesis 24,26 and 31 has made him come to conclude that what makes economic difference is not really being educated or not being educated. Repositioning oneself to have an employer mind is what makes a difference. Hence his sharing the insights on the Employer in You.